ZEN-ZEN STORIES

ZEN-ZEN STORIES

by

Edward Jurewicz

PARTRIDGE
A Penguin Random House Company

Library of Congress Control Number: 2014958220
ISBN: Hardcover   978-1-4828-2927-3
               Softcover   978-1-4828-2926-6
               eBook   978-1-4828-2928-0

To order additional copies of this book, contact
Toll Free 800 101 2657 (Singapore)
Toll Free 1 800 81 7340 (Malaysia)
orders.singapore@partridgepublishing.com

www.partridgepublishing.com/singapore

I dedicate this book to Mrs. Mana Okuya and her family, whose help in times of need was unexpected and much appreciated.

They truly embody the compassionate spirit of Buddhism!

Table of Contents

The Introduction

Like TRIVIA GAME this book offers an intellectual activity for you and your friends!

Unlike TRIVIA GAME it doesn't test your knowledge of trivial and not very useful facts! Instead, it is aimed to improve your ability to think and to express yourself. It allows you to discover more about yourself and about others. It allows you to expose and analyze your own convictions and to compare them with the opinions and the beliefs of your friends.

When we get together with our friends we often talk about trivial and unrevealing things. However, talking about the latest prices of shoes and cars, or gossiping about other people – is rather boring! This book offers a startup for interesting intellectual conversations.

Embark on this intellectual journey and begin to train your brain the way you would train your body. Think of this book as a BRAIN GYM, or a BRAIN DOJO, where you improve your skills of creative thinking, self-analysis, introspection, and debate.

You can read this book following the page order, or you can simply crack it open anywhere and read the short story that you happen to come upon. Think about it for a while. Try to interpret it in your own way. Then read the interpretation offered on the following page and answer the questions appearing at the end of the interpretation. You can also go to the very end of the book and choose one of the virtual koans to think about. You can discuss the whole thing with your friends or "exercise" in solitude. Have fun!

- The author, Edward Jurewicz.

About the author:

Edward Jurewicz has a Master's Degree in Philosophy from Carleton University, Ottawa, Canada. Following the examples of the Japanese poet – Basho, and the Korean poet – Kim Sat Gat, Edward Jurewicz chose the life of a travelling poet/writer. He has travelled the world and lived for several years in each of the following countries: Canada, Poland, Greece, Norway, South Korea, Portugal, and Japan. In Japan he has lived for 7 years so far. Edward is a vegetarian and the jacket he is wearing in the photo is synthetic! ☺

Master Hakuin's wish left at a temple.

NOT AT ALL
- STORIES

ZEN - ZEN

STORIES

Edward Jurewicz

Famous Quotes

Master Hakuin asked his disciple: "What is better – to be or not to be?"

The disciple answered: "William Shakespeare!"

Master Hakuin bowed and happily rode back to the monastery on his skateboard.

.   .   .   .   .

Mumon's comment:

Master Hakuin knows skateboarding, but in the words of Bruce Lee: "Skateboards, unlike horses, don't kick back!" One can't reasonably expect a kingdom for a skateboard!

Protecting children and offering
refuge to birds!

An Interpretation

Master Hakuin asks his student whether life is worth living, but the student only recognizes the similarity of this question to the famous words of Shakespeare: "To be or not to be..." Master Hakuin has a sense of humor, so he accepts the response of his student. He bows and "rides home on a skateboard". Serious people, such as kings or masters may ride horses, but usually don't ride skateboards, so, riding a skateboard implies humor and lightheartedness on Master Hakuin's part. Likewise, Zen stories are often humorous and lighthearted.

Mumon criticizes Master Hakuin's lighthearted response to the serious question whether existence is better than non-existence. Such a silly response is not worthy of a king, or a Zen master. Richard III wanted a horse, not a skateboard. ("A horse! A horse! My kingdom for a horse!" – Richard III, Shakespeare.)

On the other hand, by paraphrasing Bruce Lee's words ("Boards don't hit back!" – Bruce Lee in *Enter the Dragon*), Mumon comes across as not very serious either. And so, here again, the reader can get the idea that humor will play a vital role in *Zenzen Stories*. The first story suggests that Zen is not very serious and that one should read Zen stories with a pinch of salt.

Ask yourself:

1. What would you answer if Master Hakuin asked you the same question? Is life worth living? Is it better to be or not to be?

2. What famous quotes or proverbs do you use in daily life? Do you often quote famous people? If so, why? Does quoting famous people or using famous proverbs add any value to what you want to say to other people?

3. Do you ever quote the Biblical Commandments (such as: "Thou shall not lie!" or "Thou shall not steal!") or some other religious "dos and don'ts"? If so, why?

4. Zen stories are often humorous. Do you like humorous literature?

5. Do you have a funny bone in you or are you a rather serious person? How often do you joke in your daily life? (Personally I am 50/50 – half comedian, half serious or even tragic character. Sort of – *laughing through tears* kind of guy!)

6. Japanese people laugh, but they never memorize and tell jokes the way North Americans do. I once spent an entire class in front of twenty Japanese students (who spoke English well enough to understand me) telling them jokes which made me laugh. During the entire hour I was the only person laughing! Not a single Japanese person even cracked a smile! ... Canadians and Americans often smile, but my Portuguese students (yes, yes, different students! ☺) told me that smiling is not a part of their national character. Is your national character serious or light-hearted? Do people in your country often smile?

7. The dialogue in the first Zenzen story seems somewhat disjointed. Do you ever have disjointed conversations with others? Do you think that communicating with others is easy or do you often feel misunderstood?

8. Zen stories are like riddles. In order to figure out what they mean – you have to spend some time thinking about them. Do you like riddles and puzzles?

A Rude Wood

Master Hakuin and his disciples were walking along the street leading from the monastery to the village, when they came upon a local woodcutter. The woodcutter was busily sawing off a branch from a fallen tree trunk.

"Hello!" – Master Hakuin greeted the woodcutter.

"I am busy!" – responded the woodcutter angrily.

The disciples of Master Hakuin looked at the woodcutter scornfully.

"How rude is this man not to answer the greeting of our master!" – exclaimed one of the disciples.

"Don't judge him too harshly!" – said Master Hakuin. "After all it is very difficult for a tree to cut off its roots and start dancing around!"

.   .   .   .   .

Mumon's comment:

No one is free from their past. Master Hakuin can't stop teaching even when he is surrounded by a dense forest.

A Japanese monk in
Nara – begging for alms

An Interpretation

The woodcutter is a rude man, who doesn't respond to Master Hakuin's greeting with a customary greeting. The students are critical of him, but Master Hakuin explains to them that the woodcutter shouldn't be blamed, because it is not easy to shake off one's upbringing: "It is difficult for a tree to cut off its roots and start dancing around". Likewise, a human being can't easily alter the values and manners he or she grew up with.

Mumon reminds us that to overcome one's habits is hard for everyone. Even Master Hakuin can't stop being always a teacher. To be surrounded by a dense forest implies that most people, if not all, are like trees – pretty slow to change.

Ask yourself:

1. On the whole, the Japanese are a polite nation. For example: it is extremely rare for the Japanese to make obscene gestures to others (unlike in the Western countries, where drivers often show one another the middle finger). The Japanese rarely honk at other drivers. They tend to be quiet in public places. The clerks politely greet the customers in every shop, etc. Is your society on the whole rude, average, or polite? Do you often meet rude people?

2. Which countries in your opinion seem to have the most refined and polite culture and which countries seem to have the crudest culture? Why do you think nations differ in their degree of politeness?

3. Is the notion of rudeness arbitrary? For example, in one country it may be rude to publicly clean one's ears, but in another country it may be considered normal. Are there some canons of polite behavior that seem to be universal?

4. The Japanese notoriously read manga magazines in convenience stores without buying them. Is reading magazines in stores without purchasing them considered polite or appropriate in your country?

5. How do you understand the title of this story: *The Rude Wood*?

6. Does Master Hakuin seem to support tolerance? Are you a tolerant person?

7. How do you react when other people are rude to you? For example: What is your reaction when you say "good morning" and the other person doesn't respond? (Personally I say: "Ok, then NO good morning!"☺)

8. In Japan people rarely approach strangers in public places and almost never make friends with strangers on the streets. In Canada it is quite common to chitchat with a stranger at a bus stop. Is it customary in your country to talk to strangers? Have you ever talked to a stranger on the street? Is it good or bad to talk to strangers?

9. Is anger a good response to rudeness? If not, why not? What is a good response?

10. What kind of rude behavior bothers you most often in your society? (For example: crazy drivers, bossy old men, juvenile bullies, rude shopkeepers, rude customers, etc.)

Nihil Novi Sub Sole

"I have a confession to make." – said Master Hakuin to the venerable master Zensei. "I decided to write about the Buddha-nature of the world."

"What?!" – exclaimed the venerable Master Zensei. "You decided to copy me?!"

Mumon's comment:

In Japanese, Chinese, or in English; a poem, a story, a fable; now, or a thousand years ago – why does everyone copy me?!

An Interpretation

When Master Hakuin tells the venerable Master Zensei that he is writing a book on Buddhism – the latter humorously points out that it all has already been done. There are countless books on Zen Buddhism indeed.

"Nihil Novi Sub Sole" is a Latin proverb stating that *"there is nothing new under the sun"* and all things have already been done.

Mumon seems to support Master Hakuin by saying that the world's literature has already talked about all subjects. There is nothing new to say, yet new books are always being written. Another possible interpretation of Mumon's comment is that literature is universal. "Everyone copies me" may mean that literature is a universal part of human culture. Literature is relevant to people regardless of their language or culture, because it expresses human emotions and human dilemmas.

Ask yourself:

1. How often do you come across books which seem to offer nothing new and how often do you come across eye-opening books? Can you name some books which made you see the world in a different light?

2. What forms of literature do you like best and why? For example: drama, poetry, novel, short story, essay, article, etc. Do you prefer fiction or non-fiction?

3. Do you usually copy others or do you try to be original? Think about such areas as fashion, hairstyle, manicure, cooking, the manner of talking, walking, the way to spend free time, etc.

4. Are you "a copy" of your parents, your friends, or your countrymen? How much are you bound by the tradition in which you grew up? Do you try to evaluate everything by yourself or do you tend to accept the values in which you

grew up? For example: If you grew up as a Christian, can you think of Buddhism with a truly open mind? Are you willing to embrace any aspects of foreign cultures? Are you a cosmopolitan person?

5. Are other people in your society mostly original or are they mostly copycats?

6. Remember Dolly the sheep that was cloned? If a society was made up of clones, would its culture be uniform and undifferentiated? Is a diverse culture more interesting than a uniform culture? If so, why?

7. Which of your qualities would you like to pass onto your children and why?

8. Emulating a great person may be very beneficial. Whom would you recommend for other people to emulate? Whom do you emulate?

9. Can you live without other people or is contact with other people vital to you? Do you often make important decisions alone or do you usually consult with others?

10. When looking for new friends or a mate – do you prefer people who are similar to you, or people who are different from you? Explain your choice.

Hungry Chopsticks

"Snap, snap, snap" – Master Hakuin's chopsticks skillfully picked up finely chopped vegetables and rice from his bowl.

"Snap, snap, snap" – the sound of Master's chopsticks matched the speed of raindrops falling outside the window.

"Shouldn't we eat slowly in order to deeply enjoy our food?" – asked Pretty Rose somewhat scornfully.

But Master Hakuin was too busy eating to answer.

Mumon's comment:

When we chew well our digestion is better. But a hungry man enjoys his food hundredfold!

An Interpretation

Master Hakuin likes to eat fast. Eating fast is not very good for health, but it may be quite enjoyable, especially if someone is hungry.

Pretty Rose tries to correct Master Hakuin, supposedly, so that he can enjoy his food more. However, her concern seems unnecessary, since Master Hakuin is clearly enjoying his food already! Perhaps Pretty Rose wants to impose her own view of happiness on Master Hakuin, or she may have some other motives (such as the desire to keep the proper table manners), and that is why she tries to change Master Hakuin's way of eating. If she were observant enough and only concerned with Master Hakuin's happiness – she wouldn't nag.

The story seems to warn the readers against unnecessary criticism of others. In the Bible we are warned against "seeing the straw in the eyes of others and not seeing the beam in ours", that is – against being overly critical of others, while being blind to our own, greater faults.

Incidentally, monks often eat fast in order not to indulge in bodily pleasures. I remember how during my 3-month stay on Mount Athos, the Greek Orthodox monks always ate their simple meals in under five minutes, while listening to a short sermon. When I joined them for the very first meal – I barely managed to cut my bread buns open when it was time to stand up and leave the dining area. Fortunately I managed to grab the buns on my way out! From then on I have always wolfed down my food!

Ask yourself:

1. Are you a slow or a fast eater? Are you well-versed in the table manners of your country? Do you like to savor your meals, or do you usually eat to obtain nourishment rather than pleasure? Do you pay any attention to the visual presentation of your meal? Do you think that an ambiance (created by the interior decoration, music, state of cleanliness, etc.) plays an important role in the enjoyment of a meal?

2. Do you often impose your own concepts of happiness on others? Do you often give unsolicited advice to other people? Do you ever reprimand others? Do you try to change the habits of your family members? If so, how and why?

3. Are you good at giving advice to other people when asked for it? Are you sensitive to the needs of your friends? Do you ever give advice to your friends that may jeopardize their happiness? (For example: you think that your friend's boyfriend/girlfriend is not good for them, so you advise her/him to break up.)

4. Have you ever sought the advice of a professional counselor (such as a psychiatrist, priest, guru, fortune-teller, etc.)? If so, was it a successful consultation?

5. What do you think about the "professional" advisors on radio shows, who know very little about their callers' life circumstances, yet advise them to make radical changes in their lives, for example to leave their spouses? Would you ever call a radio show to seek a free, public advice about your life?

Handle of Enlightenment

In the pitch-black dungeon of Zenkoji Temple in Nagano pilgrims touch the walls looking for the Handle of Enlightenment.

While everyone else at snail-pace tried to feel their way along the walls, Master Hakuin quickly and easily led his disciples to the famous handle.

"How did he manage to find the Handle of Enlightenment so easily in the darkness?" – wondered the venerable Master Zensei upon hearing about it from the disciples.

"He used his iPhone to light up the way." – they answered.

.   .   .   .   .

Mumon's comment:

An enlightened mind finds wisdom in modern technology as well as in ancient riddles.

With his iPhone in hand Master Hakuin didn't need to leave the monastery, but his disciples were glad that he did.

Zenkoji Temple, Nagano

An Interpretation

This story is pretty much straightforward and easy to understand. Master Hakuin and his disciples visit famous Zenkoji Temple in Nagano. While in the temple, they engage in a tourist attraction – looking for an iron handle, called "the Handle of Enlightenment", which is attached to the wall in a dark underground tunnel, dramatically referred to as a "dungeon". Master Hakuin helps himself and his students using the light of his cell-phone.

Mumon praises Master Hakuin for employing modern technology in the symbolic search for wisdom. Instead of "feeling the walls" in the darkness, Master Hakuin invents the proverbial light bulb and lights up the way to enlightenment with his phone. Of course many traditionally minded people would think of Master Hakuin's method as cheating.

Modern technology can be very useful indeed and it may even become a substitute for travelling by providing us with the ability to discover the world virtually – on the internet, without leaving home. Nevertheless, the students are happy to have gone to Zenkoji Temple with their teacher.

On a personal note, all of my Japanese students disapproved of Master Hakuin's cunning use of the iPhone light... "But you know, the man in front of me had a runny nose and he coughed a lot. I banged into him a few times in the darkness before I finally turned on my iPhone's flashlight..." – explained Master Hakuin.

Ask yourself:

1. Was Master Hakuin smart to use his iPhone or was he a cheater?

2. Have you ever cheated on a school test? Is cheating on school tests a mark of intelligence or is it simply an immoral and unacceptable conduct?

3. What is the average school test designed to check – the students' understanding of a subject or the students' memory? Are the typical school tests reliable in checking the students' educational progress?

4. What was the real Handle of Enlightenment for Master Hakuin – the iron handle attached to the wall or his iPhone?

5. New inventions often radically change the way in which we interact with the world. Name a few inventions which permanently replaced their predecessors. For example – a washing machine permanently replaced a washboard; a phone replaced a messenger pigeon ☺, etc.

6. Does modern technology help us discover the world? If so, how?

7. Do you prefer to sightsee virtually or in real life? Explain your preference.

8. Does modern technology have an impact on religion and spirituality? If so, in what way? What do you think about televangelism?

9. In Japan many Buddhist temples have satellite dishes mounted on their roofs. Do you think that monks need satellite TV? Of course in Japan many Buddhist priests are not monks. Many priests are married and have normal family life.

The Solitude of Life

When Master Hakuin fell ill – he decided to go into seclusion.

"I will be alone for some time until I recover... or die!" – Master Hakuin said to his disciples.

"Master, you mustn't say such things! Of course you will recover!" – the disciples cried out.

"Only a fool cries when a rainbow dies!" – responded Master Hakuin and smiled.

.   .   .   .   .

Mumon's comment:

A rainbow is alone, but is it ever lonely?

Master Hakuin is an old dog. He knows full well that in order to recover he must lick his wounds in hiding.

Feeling blue

An Interpretation

One of the main topics in this story is solitude. Humans are social beings and most of us dislike being alone for a long time. However, spending some time alone is often extremely important to our well-being. When an animal gets sick, it often goes into hiding and tries to recover alone. Similarly, Master Hakuin wants to be alone when he doesn't feel well.

Master Hakuin's disciples worry about their master's state of health. However, Master Hakuin reminds them that one should remain calm and stoic in the face of life's calamities. Being sick and even dying – are natural events, just like the disappearance of a rainbow, and one should not despair if they happen to take place. Of course thinking of death with a stoic attitude is not easy and one really has to be a Zen master to acquire such a state of mind.

Mumon suggests in his comment that Master Hakuin isn't really contemplating his death yet. (Of course Zenzen Stories are just beginning, so Master Hakuin cannot possibly die yet! ☺) He just wants the disciples not to worry and not to bother him for a while. Being alone isn't always synonymous with being lonely. A rainbow is usually alone in the sky, yet it is always colorful and happy – as it indicates the transition from a rainy weather to a sunny one.

Loneliness, sickness, and death are not easy to deal with, and so the story doesn't really offer any advice, but only hints at courage and acceptance of the facts of nature.

Ask yourself:

1. Do you often spend time alone? Do you feel that you need to be alone at times? How does being alone benefit you? How does socializing with other people benefit you? What do you usually do when you are alone?

2. While being alone is often beneficial, it isn't always easy. Many people dislike being alone and try to cover up the feeling of loneliness by watching television or listening to the radio. Can you spend time without looking at or listening to other people? Why, do you think, most people dislike being alone?

3. Is it better to surround yourself with real, but boring friends, or with interesting fictional characters from books and movies? Can book authors, movie makers and other artists become your friends even if you never meet them in person or connect with them by phone or mail? Would you rather talk about the price of shoes with someone in the same room or would you prefer to engage in an interesting "conversation" with an artist by contemplating his/her artwork?

4. What do you usually do when you get sick – do you seek help of other people or do you try to stay away from everyone?

5. Can Zazen meditation help in learning to cope with loneliness?

6. Are you always alone, sometimes alone, or never alone in life?

7. Is it important for children to spend time alone and without any distraction of TV, computer games, or even books? If so, why?

The Power of Zen Stories

Josei asked Master Hakuin:

"Why are Zen stories always so short?"

Master Hakuin responded:

"A long tale is like a tongue of a buffalo – chewing grass and licking its own nostrils. A Zen story is like a sting of a bee – it's quick and very painful!

.   .   .   .   .

Mumon's comment:

A bear in search of honey must often bear a sting of a bee. But beware of the Japanese killer hornet. Its message is more poignant than a bite of a viper!

Beware!

An Interpretation

A Japanese killer hornet can be a really vicious bugger. A few months after my arrival in Japan I was stung by one! It came to me from its underground nest as I was approaching the area of its residence with my dogs. It came fast and without any hesitation it went straight for my leg. I had never seen such a fearless insect before! The pain was severe, as if someone had driven a nail into my leg! I screamed, called off my dogs, and retreated instantly. I didn't go to a doctor, though I was told later that it could have been lethal. In Japan more people die every year from a killer hornet's sting than from a bite of a viper. It took a week or so for my leg to stop being inflamed.

Zen stories can be likened to a serious bite or a sting, because they are meant to shake us up and alter our perception of the world. Ideally, they can bring about some kind of illumination, or satori.

Of course at times long literary works may be extremely revealing or illuminating. Such masterpieces as Shakespeare's *Hamlet*, Dostoyevsky's *Brothers Karamazov*, Nietzsche's *Thus Spoke Zarathustra*, or Kierkegaard's *Either/Or* – are nothing like "a long tongue of a buffalo licking its own nostrils." They are never verbose or boring. Nonetheless, the beauty of most Zen stories lies in their concise nature. Just like haiku poetry – composed of only 17 syllables, or like Japanese meals – small, but full of colors, textures and flavors – Zen anecdotes are meant to excite by being succinct and thought-provoking. The reader of a Zen story should want to create the rest of the story in his or her mind.

Ask yourself:

1. Do you like short or long literary forms better? Think of the reasons for your preference. (Personally, my short-attention span makes me favor short literary forms! I wish we could communicate complex ideas in simple words!)

2. Do you tend to talk too much or are you a quiet type? Have you ever tried to be silent for a day? If not, do you think you could do it?

3. Why do you usually talk? A. To show how smart you are. B. To convey a message. (Men are said to often talk for this reason.) C. To connect emotionally with another person. (Women are said to often talk for this reason.) D. To cheer up or to entertain other people. E. For some other reason.

4. Our interaction with the world of insects is usually very limited. Most people don't have much to do with insects except when they are bugged by bugs and when they try to get rid of them. The Buddhists monks and nuns try to be compassionate even towards insects. When you see a fly, a butterfly, or an ant – do you try to be gentle toward it? Have you ever saved a drowning insect from a puddle?

5. Short literary forms, such as short stories or short poems, tend to be difficult to understand. Perhaps it was Kilgore Trout who wrote the following poem: "I get hiccups at the D-cups and my favorite animals are Z-bras." ☺ ... Or maybe it was Master Hakuin when he was young? Anyway, do you find it amusing or just silly?

A Wake-up Call

Master Hakuin woke up at 3 a.m. and put on his robes. However, he made so much commotion while dressing up that all of his disciples sleeping in the adjacent rooms also woke up.

"Is it already time to meditate, Master?" – asked the surprised disciples.

"I just ate too much bread before going to bed!" – answered Master Hakuin. He grabbed a roll of toilet paper and a flashlight – and left the retirement quarters of the monastery.

.   .   .   .   .

Mumon's comment:

In the middle of the night a stomachache makes Master Hakuin wake up his disciples.

He is a true master indeed!

An Interpretation

The concept of "awakening" (or "waking up") plays the pivotal role in this story. In Buddhist terminology to "awaken someone" means to bring someone to enlightenment or satori. Hence, a Zen master always tries to awaken his disciples. Master Hakuin's nightly trip to the toilet wakes up his disciples and that is why Mumon calls Master Hakuin "a true master". Of course waking up someone physically is not synonymous with a spiritual awakening.

Sometimes Zen stories talk about pretty unrefined topics. The story about Master Hakuin's trip to the toilet in the middle of the night – is one of such unrefined stories.

Do you remember the famous Zen story titled *Dry Dung*? The story goes like this: A monk asked Ummon: "What is Buddha?" Ummon answered: "Dried dung." This is an old and well-known story published in *Zen Flesh, Zen Bones* collection. Buddha is likened to dried dung, because Buddha (or Buddha-nature) is everywhere! Buddha-nature is present in the stars in the sky, as well as in the dew drops on the grass. It is present in the most developed creatures, as well as in the "lowly" worms. It is present in everything, including dung. Nothing exists outside of the realm of Buddha. Since Buddha is all encompassing – therefore all existence is praiseworthy. In fact, worms are not lowly at all, and even dung may be regarded with reverence.

Do you know dung beetles or scarabs? Dung beetles can be often seen pushing a ball of dung. In ancient Egypt scarabs were viewed as the representations of God and the ball of dung they push was thought to be the miniature representation of the sun in the sky. And so dung beetles and balls of dung were treated as divine by the ancient Egyptians and often depicted in jewelry and other forms of art.

In *Dried Dung* koan Ummon tells us that there is nothing disgusting or unworthy in nature. The power of this famous koan lies in the juxtaposition of Buddha and dried dung. In Master Hakuin's story there is a similar juxtaposition of the students' expectation – that their master wakes them up for a Zazen practice, and the reality – that the master needs to use the toilet.

Ask yourself:

1. Do you tend to be squeamish when it comes to unrefined topics, or can you read and talk about any such topic without feeling uncomfortable?

2. Do you think that nature is divine (it has Buddha quality) or created by God? If so, is all nature praiseworthy or are some parts of nature disgusting, vile, and "good for nothing"? For example – what do you think about ants? Are ants useless or divine? How about such parasites as tapeworms or flatworms? Is it possible to think of fungus with reverence?

3. Childbirth is accompanied by blood, mucus, birth water, and placenta. Do you think of a birth of a human or an animal as clean or dirty?

4. When I lived in Korea I spent some time with my Taekwondo teacher, his wife and their baby. I remember how the baby boy peed on his mother's hands, and the mother didn't wash her hands, but only dried them in a towel. Serving me food (without washing her hands) she explained that her baby's urine was very clean... Hmmm... I wasn't convinced. Is human waste clean or dirty?

5. Does the contrast between the expectation of the disciples (who think it's time to meditate) and the reality (Master Hakuin's need to go to the toilet) seem humorous to you? Have you ever experienced a big gap between your expectations and reality? If so, on what occasion? I remember how one night I was laughing in my dream and my father woke me up comforting me, because he thought that I had been crying...

6. Do you think that there is a big difference between our expectations when we first get involved in a romantic

relationship and the reality that becomes more and more obvious over the years?

7. Are you familiar with Kafka's story titled *Metamorphosis*? If so, were you disgusted by the image of a man who becomes a beetle? Of course human body is far more familiar to us than that of a beetle, but if you try to be objective in your judgment, which body is more elegant: the hard and shiny exoskeleton of a beetle or the soft and often flabby flesh of a human?

8. Would Kafka's story be equally revolting and shocking if a beetle were to become a human being? If not, why not?

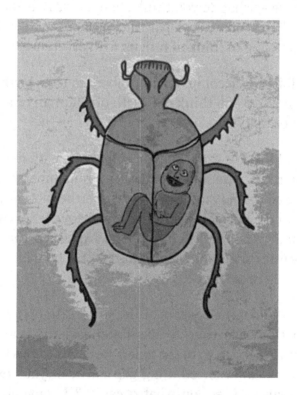

A Kafkaesque beetle carrying
a human child inside.

Platonic Love Doesn't Prickle

In Ancient Greece it was customary for older male teachers to have young male students as lovers. What a strange custom!

Plato was a wrestling champion of Athens. He was young, smart, strong, and very handsome. He offered himself as a lover to his teacher – Socrates – who was old and ugly. However, Socrates rejected Plato, and so the term "platonic love" (non-physical love) was coined.

When Pretty Rose asked Master Hakuin to marry her – he gave her a book by Plato in response.

. . . . .

Mumon's comment:

Master Hakuin was too old! Pretty Rose would have made a good fourth wife, if only she had no thorns and a chronically runny nose.

An Interpretation

The etymology of the term "platonic love" may seem interesting to the readers, but what is the main point of this story? Master Hakuin rejects Pretty Rose's proposal just like Socrates rejected Plato's advances. Master Hakuin doesn't want to complicate his relationship with Pretty Rose. What exactly is their relationship? From this and other stories in the book we may deduce that it is more than just a teacher/student relationship. Are they in love with each other? Or perhaps they are just very good friends? In either case, Mumon seems to think that Master Hakuin should have accepted the proposal, even though Pretty Rose is not without vices. And neither, of course, is Master Hakuin!

As the picture below illustrates – romantic relationships are hard to deal with. Perhaps Master Hakuin's relationship with Pretty Rose is not platonic after all, but Master Hakuin is not ready to make a life-time commitment. Especially since it looks like he had already been married (three times!) in the past.

It is interesting to notice that great spiritual leaders are often single, or if married, they are frequently regarded as negligent spouses and parents. Mahatma Gandhi, for instance, admitted to being inattentive towards his wife and children. Gandhi's spousal and parental shortcomings were undoubtedly caused by his sense of responsibility for the good of the entire nation.

Siddhartha Gautama Buddha also chose to seek enlightenment and find the way to help all the suffering beings rather than to care for his immediate family. To care more for the good of the nation than for one's own immediate family is "the curse" of many great political, social, and spiritual leaders.

Ask yourself:

1. Do you think that being a leader of a large social group is compatible with being a good spouse or a good parent? If not, why not?

2. According to the majority of "cops and robbers" movies – good police officers are often divorced. Why do you think it is so? What other jobs are incompatible (or hard to handle) with marriage and raising children? (For example: sailor, long-distance truck driver, pop-star, religious leader, international journalist, etc.)

3. The pope and the catholic priests cannot marry. On one hand it allows them to focus on the good of all people, but on the other hand it may cause some sexual frustrations. The protestant priests and the Zen teachers can and often do marry, but Buddhist monks and nuns remain celibate. Should priests and spiritual teachers be allowed to marry?

4. Do you remember the movie *Seven Year's Itch* with Marilyn Monroe? Some people believe that married people naturally lose the excitement about their spouses after 7 years. One German politician (Gabriele Pauli of Christian Social Union in Bavaria) suggested that all marriages should be automatically dissolved after 7 years. Those who want to continue being married after 7 years should then request the extension of their marriage. What do you think about this idea?

5. A Danish philosopher Søren Kierkegaard wrote: "If you get married – you will regret it. If you don't get married – you will regret it. Whether you get married or you don't get married – you will regret it." How do you understand these words? Do you agree with Kierkegaard? Is it difficult to be married or to live with someone?

6. Can you interpret the following picture titled *Relationship*?

Relationship

7. Is it educational to be a parent? What can parents learn from the experience of raising children?

8. Vincent Van Gogh, Nietzsche, Kierkegaard, Michelangelo, Beethoven, Plato, Chopin, Matsuo Basho, Jean-Paul Sartre, Simone de Beauvoir, Virginia Woolf, and Jane Austen are some of the famous artists who had no children. On the other hand, Leo Tolstoy had 13 children. Johan Sebastian Bach had 20 children (of whom only 10 survived to adulthood). Alexandre Dumas (father) was one of the most prolific writers of all times. He is said to have written over 270 books and to have fathered at least four children (all of whom were out of wedlock). Should great artists have children? Do the artists with children have different things to say from the artists who have never experienced parenthood?

Buddha's Nostril

In Todaiji Temple in Nara pilgrims try to fit through the nostril of the Giant Buddha Statue. If one can do it – it is said to guarantee a good afterlife for that person.

When Master Hakuin visited Nara – he tried to pass through the Buddha's nostril too. Unfortunately his chest was simply too broad for the task.

"Will Master Hakuin not have a good afterlife?" – asked Mondai.

"Of course he won't!" – answered Master Kotae.

"But he is such a compassionate and kind man!" – exclaimed Mondai. "Why should he not have a good rebirth?"

"That's precisely the reason." – answered Master Kotae. "His chest is too big and so is his heart!"

Mumon's comment:

A good rebirth is better than a bad rebirth, but can Buddha pass through his own nostril?

Todaiji Giant Buddha

The Giant Buddha is cast in bronze and it is the largest bronze Buddha statue in the world. Todaiji means *Great Eastern Temple*. The temple and the Giant Buddha were built in Nara period (710-794 C.E.) in Nara city at the order of Emperor Shomu, who was a devout Buddhist.

An Interpretation

We are told that the founder of Buddhism – Gautama Siddhartha Buddha – was a prince, who lived in India in about 500 B.C. His father was very protective of him, so Gautama grew up in a palace, in a safe and beautiful environment, and he was never exposed to any harshness or cruelty of life. He married young – at the age of 16, and soon he and his young wife got a child. The three of them lived happily for a while. One day Gautama was wandering on the streets outside the palace and he saw three scenes that shocked him and changed his life. He saw a sick person, an old person, and a dead body. Upon witnessing these shocking and painful scenes Gautama realized that life was not as happy as he had previously imagined. As a result of this realization at the age of 29 Gautama abandoned his family and went on a spiritual quest to find the way to escape suffering. For a few years he studied with yogis and ascetics, but in the end he discovered his own path to freedom from suffering. When he became 35 years old he became "fully awakened" and soon after he started to teach his philosophy to others.

Buddha came to believe that life filled with suffering was not worth living, and non-existence was better! But according to the belief in which Buddha grew up (Hinduism) – there was reincarnation or life after life. If we try to escape life's suffering by committing suicide, we will be reborn without having learned this life's lesson and so we will probably suffer even more as a result of our misguided action. If we really want to escape suffering, we have to do it differently. We must extinguish our desires. According to Buddhism, there are 108 desires and we should try to eradicate them all. If we manage to do it – we will achieve Nirvana – the state of non-existence, and we will not be born into suffering again.

Since Master Hakuin cannot pass through the nostril of the Buddha statue perhaps he won't have a good rebirth. But according to Buddhism – Nirvana or non-existence – is better than any rebirth. Master Kotae seems to think that Master Hakuin's big heart makes him similar to Buddha and ready for Nirvana.

Ask yourself:

1. What desires seem to be the strongest in you? For example: a desire for good food, sweets and desserts, for coffee or other stimulating drinks, a desire for alcohol, for sex, for luxury or money, a desire to rest and be lazy, a desire to be respected by others, to be loved by others, a desire for knowledge, a desire to experience novelty or change, a desire for adventure, for health, for physical or emotional strength, for longevity, a desire to be safe from harm, a desire to have a beautiful or handsome romantic partner, to have a happy family, a desire to help others, to make the world a better place, etc.

2. Would you like to get rid of all desires if you were sure that it would prevent you from suffering in the future? Personally, I like many of my desires even at the cost of some suffering. Of course I am afraid of severe or extensive suffering!...

3. If you had to choose between being reborn on a happy planet where no one is suffering or on the planet Earth where you can help other beings – what would you choose and why?

4. Isn't the hope to escape suffering also a desire? If it is, should we eradicate it? What happens if we eradicate the desire to achieve Nirvana?

5. It is written in the Bible: "If your right hand offends you, cut it off and throw it away." Matthew 5:30. In Tolstoy's story titled *Father Sergius* the main character cuts off his finger to protect himself from the seduction of a woman. Do you think that sexual desires are evil? Should we protect ourselves from adultery by such drastic measures as cutting off our body parts?

6. Do you often fight with your desires? If so, how? Do you have a strong will? Is it difficult for you to keep your New Year's resolutions?

This hole in the pillar in Todaiji temple represents the Great Buddha's nostril.

The River of Now

One day Master Hakuin and Pretty Rose went to the river. As they sat down on the bank of the river, Pretty Rose said:

"I wonder what vegetables I should cook tomorrow for dinner..."

Master Hakuin responded:

"How about a soup of river water with a handful of grass?"

.   .   .   .   .

Mumon's comment:

When you are in the mountains – touch the clouds and listen to the blowing winds. When you are by the river – wet your feet and feel the grass growing between your fingers. And when you are in the desert – think about cooking dinner and vacuuming your house.

Enjoy!

An Interpretation

One of the main teachings of Zen Buddhism is to live in the PRESENT MOMENT. But what exactly does it mean?

Many people get caught up in planning and thinking about the future, even the most basic or trivial future, such as preparing the meal for the next day, instead of noticing their present circumstances.

Ok, perhaps meals are not trivial. In fact they are pretty important! Meals are important for various reasons – such as making your spouse happy or simply staying healthy. But when you are spending time outdoors, in some refreshing, scenic, natural environment – it's good to forget about the dinner for a while and just contemplate the beauty around you!

In this story, Master Hakuin tells Pretty Rose to make a dish out of the river water and the grass in order to make her focus on the surrounding beauty. Mumon adds that one should not think of mundane tasks such as household chores (cooking or vacuuming) unless one is in a mundane or boring environment, symbolically represented by a desert. Of course in real life a desert may also offer a very interesting experience, especially when it is seen for the first time!

Do you remember the flower you saw last? How many petals did it have? Do you remember where it was growing? Do you remember the color of that flower? No? How about the color of your best friend's sweater when you met him or her last time?

You may think that the details of what you see, hear, smell, taste, or touch are not very important. After all, what is the difference if the flower you see is red or yellow, or if the tea you drink is mint, green, or earl grey? But actually paying attention to the details enhances your experiences and makes you appreciate them more. Your appreciation of what you experience in life is what makes all the difference. Happiness is a state of mind.

Overall – keep your senses sharp and look at things from different angles. Just like a painter who creates the reality on canvas, try to create your experiences on the canvas of your mind. It's not so much what is out there, but how you see it – that counts! It's up to you to make your life a living and changing masterpiece!

When you sit on the bank of the river, do you feel the fingers of the grass gently caressing your legs?

Ask yourself:

1. Are you an observant person? Without turning around describe what is behind you. Then see if you remembered it well.

2. Are you focused on the present moment? Do you appreciate it? Think why this present moment is beneficial to you.

3. Saving money may indicate that you are deeply focused on the future, while spending money on daily basis usually means that you are more focused on the present moment. Do you tend to be a penny pincher or a spendthrift? Which is better and why?

4. Do you know the fable about an idle grasshopper and a diligent ant? In the summer the grasshopper enjoyed his life idly, but the ant worked hard every day. In the winter the grasshopper was hungry, but the ant had plenty of food supplies. What is the moral of this story? Which insect lived more for the future and which one lived more in the present? Does Zen promote idleness?

5. Can one be a responsible parent living merely in the passing moment?

6. Without thinking about the future one couldn't have any goal in mind. For example, one wouldn't study Buddhism without having enlightenment or self-improvement in mind. Since to

complete any task one must remember the past and expect the future, what does living in the present moment really mean?

7. Think about and enumerate all the blessings in your present life. For example – being alive, not being in great pain, having friends, living in a relatively good country, etc.

8. People with a positive attitude to life tend to feel happier than those who are always negative. Due to the power of positive thinking they also tend to be healthier and live longer than those who are bitter and unhappy. Are you a positive person?

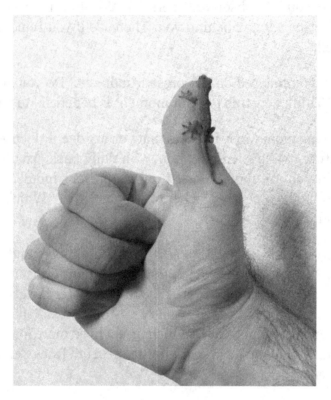

Thumbs up!

Understanding Individualism

"All flowers face in one direction, but one flower faces in the opposite direction. Is this what individualism is about?" – asked Mondai.

"Washing your bowl well before filling it with new rice – that's what individualism is about!" – replied Master Hakuin.

.   .   .   .   .

Mumon's comment:

Master Hakuin understood Mondai's deep hunger. It is said that a man thinks better on a full stomach.

But truly, individualism is not a rejection of the commonly accepted values, but rather their unbiased evaluation. Mondai should not only wash his bowl but also cook his own rice!

Should he also become a farmer?

An Interpretation

The metaphor of emptying one's cup before filling it with new food or drink has been used in many Zen stories. In order to fully embrace the teachings of Zen, one has to first get rid of the previously acquired philosophies and beliefs. In other words, one should face Buddhism with an open mind and heart and without any prejudice.

In Christianity the idea of cleansing one's heart and mind before fully embracing the teachings of Jesus is also well known. Meister Eckhart and other Christian mystics say that one must get rid of the ego in order to let God fill one's heart and mind with the Divine Will.

In philosophy – we are generally told to think for ourselves and never accept any ideas without a thorough evaluation. And that is what individualism is all about!

In the story, Mondai asks if individualism is synonymous with being different from others. A single flower facing in the direction opposite to all the other flowers – seems to be independent and self-relying. But Master Hakuin tells Mondai that opposing the majority is not necessarily a mark of independence or self-reliance. Sometimes people who reject the values or ideas accepted by others do so only in order to be defiant or to come across as rebels. A mark of true independence and individualism is being an unbiased judge of all beliefs and not accepting or rejecting any belief on the basis of what other people choose or think. Master Hakuin tells Mondai to evaluate the world by himself – to make his own choices and to forge his own opinions, regardless of others.

It is difficult to be a true individualist, because we grow up in societies and soak in their values, ideas, and beliefs. Hence, to be a true individualist we may have to not only "clean our bowls between meals, but also cook our own meals, and perhaps even grow our own food". We may need to distance ourselves from the cultural baggage we receive from the societies in which we grow up. But is it ever possible?

Ask yourself:

1. Most people are very conventional in what they wear. For example: they never go ballroom dancing in sandals or in slippers, and they never put on unmatched socks. Extravagant behavior is expected of famous artists, yet normal people are judged negatively if they wear strange clothes (for example: Elton John type hats and glasses, or a single glove like Michael Jackson). Do you care about what other people think of your fashion? Do you ever act in unconventional or daring ways?

2. Many people never change the beliefs with which they grow up. What is your parents' religion? Is your religion the same? What beliefs and values acquired in childhood did you question when you became older? Are there any differences in values between you and your parents? For example: my parents were not vegetarians, but I am.

3. If your values or convictions are different from the values and convictions of the society you live in – do you tend to hide those differences, or do you emphasize them? For example: if you live in a Christian society, but you are a Buddhist, do you tell other people about your beliefs, or do you keep quiet about them? Do you think it is better to hide your beliefs if they are unusual?

4. Do other people often think of you as a *strange person*, or do they usually think of you as an *average* or *normal person*?

5. In Japan there is a saying: "A nail that sticks out gets hammered down." What do you think it means?

6. Do you live in an obedient society where conformity abounds or is your society rebellious and individualistic?

7. What are the pros and the cons of living among individualists?

Being Different

(This single sunflower was really growing this way!)

The Peach and the Bamboo Straw

One day Master Hakuin and Pretty Rose went to the river again. In the bushes on the river's bank Master Hakuin picked up a bamboo straw and started to whittle a flute out of it. As soon as he cut the bamboo – a little girl jumped out of it.

At that moment Pretty Rose noticed a peach floating down the river.

"There must be a little boy inside that peach!" – she exclaimed excitedly.

And so Master Hakuin, Pretty Rose, and their two children were a happy family for one day.

Mumon's comment:

To understand this story one doesn't need to know the Japanese folklore, but rather one needs to be a man or a woman for a while.

An Interpretation

Despite Mumon's comment, this story might be hard to understand unless you know the traditional Japanese folk tales. The story has references to two famous folktales: *Hime – the Bamboo Princess* and *Momotaro – the Peach Boy*. As the titles already give away – Hime was a princess born out of a bamboo and Momotaro was a boy born out of a peach. What I find interesting in these stories is that the bamboo and the peach can be seen as the symbols of male and female sexuality. Hence, the bonds between father (bamboo) and his daughter, and mother (peach) and her son are emphasized.

In the Western folklore, vegetation and other elements of nature are also often used to symbolize human sexuality. The most famous of all natural symbols is the apple. The Biblical forbidden fruit represents knowledge of good and evil, and of eternal life. How do we acquire knowledge? – Through experiences in life. And how do we get to "live forever"? – Through our offspring. Both – knowledge and eternal life are closely connected with birth and of course with motherhood. Female breasts are often portrayed as apples in the European symbolic art. The Biblical snake, on the other hand, can be seen as the representation of male sexuality. Moses and the Egyptian magicians were able to change their staffs into snakes. Staffs, snakes, swords, and scepters – are all used in the Western folklore and culture as symbols of male fertility. Medieval European kings used both – male and female symbols to display their power. In one hand they would hold a scepter (a short staff) and in the other hand they would hold a royal orb (or a royal apple). The scepter/staff represented the king's rule and it was connected with male power. The orb/apple represented the reign over the land – and it was connected with female power. Even king Arthur's sword – stuck in a rock, was originally forged in Avalon – the legendary land of apple trees.

Fruits, vegetables, and other elements of nature (such as snakes or shells) – often inspire people to compare them to human sexual organs and one doesn't have to be a Freudian to see the connection.

Ask yourself:

1. What fruits or vegetables are used as symbols of human sexuality in your culture?

2. What is your favorite fruit or vegetable and why? Are there any fruits or vegetables you dislike?

3. If you were to compare yourself (including your mind, body, character, etc.) to a fruit or a vegetable – what fruit or vegetable would you be most similar to? ☺

4. Although in Ancient Greece sexuality had been freely expressed, due to the later influence of Christianity in most Western countries sexuality has been historically a taboo subject. In Japan, as a result of the leniency and tolerance of Buddhism and Shintoism sexuality has been more openly accepted. For example, "love hotels" are quite numerous in Japan and used by almost all Japanese. Do you feel shy about sexuality? What is your opinion about the sexual education (in schools, or on the radio, or TV) in your country?

5. "Too much sexual freedom may lead us to Sodom and Gomorrah!" Do you think so? Explain your opinion. Should young people have access to explicit sex images on the internet?

6. Is there a difference between erotic art and pornography? What is the difference? What do you think about abusive pornography? Is pornography educational? Can pornography play a healing role, or is it only a mind warping and degenerating stimulant?

7. What is your opinion about prostitution?

8. Do you believe in monogamous or polygamous relationships? Should a person have more than one intimate partner in their lifetime?

9. How can you interpret the following painting titled *The Shadows of Beauty*?

The Shadows of Beauty

Mumon's Comments

When Master Hakuin read some of his Zen stories to the venerable Master Zensei, the latter said:

"Mumon's comments seem to complicate rather than to explain the stories."

Master Hakuin responded:

"Mumon's comments are the budding leaves on the branches."

Mumon's comment:

No comment.

An Interpretation

In this very short story Master Zensei accuses Mumon of being obscure and making the stories more complex rather than explaining their meaning. Master Zensei is right! Zen stories are traditionally very short. Each story is often composed of a short question and answer. Traditionally in a Zen story the commentator adds "foliage" to the presented picture and makes the story more colorful. In many Zen stories Mumon offers his poems. Mumon's poems are doubly difficult to understand – not only because they are Zen riddles, but also because they are written in a vague poetical language. Although Master Hakuin likes poetry – he decided against it in Zenzen Stories (except for a few funny poems he wrote as a young man... or perhaps it was Kilgore Trout ☺). Obscurity is a virtue only when it prompts the audience to partake in the process of creation. When obscurity overwhelms and discourages – it becomes an unnecessary hindrance.

The complaint of Master Zensei may instigate us to think about the role of communication in art, and more generally, about the role of art. According to Aristotle, literary art has three functions: to educate, to inspire or move emotionally, and to delight or entertain. Personally I would add at least one more function – which is to turn the readers into creators. The most popular books are those that do just that. Kafka's *The Trial*, Nietzsche's *Thus Spoke Zarathustra*, and Camus's *The Stranger* – are extremely popular not **despite** their obscurity, but **because of it**, and because they all require creative involvement on the part of the readers. They are like colorful Play-Doh tempting children to become sculptors.

Ask yourself:

1. What is, in your opinion, the most important function of literature? Why?

2. What kind of books do you like to read most (educational, inspirational, entertaining, or challenging the reader's

creativity)? Name a few of your favorite books. (You may include this one! ☺) What do you like about them?

3. The main difference between studying science (for example math) and studying art (for example literature) is that science usually requires one correct answer, while in art many answers are correct. While 2 plus 2 can only be 4 (in accordance with the standard math), many interpretations of a literary work are correct! Of course some interpretations are more interesting than others; nonetheless the freedom of interpretation in art is much greater than the freedom of finding the proper answer in science. Do you prefer to study science or art? Why?

4. Do you prefer to read facts or fiction? Is there such a thing as "historical facts", or "scientific facts", or are so called "facts" also only opinions? An opinion is a subjective interpretation of reality and it is not necessarily true. For example: for a long time people believed that the sun revolved around the Earth. They believed not in a fact, but only in an opinion of some scientists (like Ptolemy and Aristotle).

5. Do you like to be creative? What kind of creative activities do you engage in? (For example: interpreting literature, cooking, choosing fashionable clothes, decorating your room, writing a journal, painting, telling lies or tall tales, etc.)

The Nature of Beauty

One day Mondai asked the venerable Master Zensei about the nature of beauty:

"There are many beautiful sights we can admire every day, such as Mount Fuji, the ocean, beautiful flowers and beautiful women. But what can we admire in the darkness of the night?"

"The mu..." – answered the venerable Master Zensei.

"Yes! Mu - Nothingness!" – exclaimed Mondai happily clapping his hands in excitement. Mondai was glad to have asked such a wise question that yielded a profound answer, so he went to Master Hakuin and told him about the encounter with Master Zensei.

"You misunderstood!" – said Master Hakuin. "The venerable Master Zensei often stutters. He wanted to say not "mu" but "the moon"!"

.   .   .   .   .

Mumon's comment:

Beauty is not what **is** but what we **want it to be**. Even the most beautiful woman has sleepy eyes, bad breath, and pimples – on occasion.

The Beauty and the Beast

An Interpretation

Much of the Japanese cultural heritage is genuinely beautiful. The extensive use of a powerful color combination: black, red, and white, as well as the unique design of the traditional houses and temples make the Japanese architecture truly admirable. The Japanese gardens with their carp-filled ponds, ikebana (the art of flower arrangement), the shapes and the patterns of the traditional kimonos, yukatas and jimbeys (Japanese summer clothes), handheld fans, origami (paper decorations), and various personal and household ornaments – seem beautiful to most people, regardless of their cultural background.

However, some of what is perceived as beautiful by the Japanese is completely inaccessible to foreign minds. It is so, because for the Japanese beauty lies also in adherence to the established rules.

Take for example calligraphy. What is a beautiful stroke of a brush as opposed to an ugly one? Only a person skilled in the art of calligraphy may tell the difference.

Haiku poetry may not be easily appreciated by an ignorant foreigner. Three lines composing a poem may carry less meaning than a splash of a carp in a pond. Rhyming is strictly forbidden in haiku poetry... hence, here again beauty lies in the adherence to the precise number of syllables and in expressing some observation about life in very few words.

The beauty of the tea ceremony depends on the precise movements of the host as well as the guests. The way to handle the spoon filled with tea, to mix the tea and water with a brush and pour the tea into the cup, as well as the way to turn the cup before drinking, and finally to admire the craftsmanship of the empty cup – may be studied and mastered for years. The more one knows the etiquette the more beautifully one behaves. The elusive beauty of following the rules is of course present in many cultures, but in Japan it seems to have reached truly grand proportions.

Ask yourself:

1. What is beautiful to you? Name five objects, or elements of nature that come to mind when you think of something beautiful.

2. Is beauty universal – are the same features appreciated all over the world?

3. Is beauty objective or subjective? Do you usually agree with the judges of beauty contests or with your friends when talking about attractive looking people? Is your sense of beauty average or unusual?

4. Tastes and preferences often change in the course of life. For example, most children like desserts and fruit juice best, but as adults they may prefer spicy foods and beer. Similarly, human perception of beauty changes over time. What fashions, hair styles, idols, and images of beauty did you admire in the past, which you no longer admire? (E. g., long hair on men, bell-bottom pants, hippie style clothes, the looks of Elvis Presley and Marilyn Monroe, etc.)

5. The ancient Greeks thought that beauty had to do with symmetry. Do you think that symmetry is more appealing to the eye than lack of symmetry? The basic rule of ikebana calls for an asymmetrical arrangement. Is ikebana aesthetically attractive to you or is it ugly?

6. Describe the features of a handsome man or a beautiful woman. Think of some famous people as examples of beauty. Compare your opinion with the opinion of others. Is your perception of beauty similar to the perception of others?

7. Does beauty depend on inner qualities? Can an ignorant man or an evil woman be handsome or beautiful? Can a good person, whose looks seem average at first glance, become beautiful to you when you get to know his or her character?

8. Perhaps the way we see beauty in humans is connected with youth, health, vigor and the ability to produce the best offspring? Perhaps we are most attracted to people who (we think) carry the best DNA for the future generations to inherit?

9. Perhaps beautiful fruits are those which (we think) are the most delicious and nutritious? Describe a beautiful apple. Is it unripe, overripe, or just ripe and perfect for consumption?

10. Every country has its own style of architecture and interior design. Which countries architecture and interior design do you like best and why?

11. The traditional Japanese interior design is simple and bare. Many Western interior designs are very complex. What impact on the mind does simplicity have? Do you like collecting trinkets? Is your home messy or clean?

12. Can you interpret the following picture titled *Emptiness*?

EMPTINESS

Sitting in Zazen

Sitting in the lotus position Suatte said to himself:

"I must remain motionless till noon!"

At 11:58 someone called out: "Suatte! Suatte!"

Suatte did not respond.

The calling intensified: "Suatte! Suatte! Open the door!"

Suatte looked at the clock. The seconds were passing so slowly! It was still 11:58.

"Suatte, for crying out loud! It's me – your teacher! Open the door right now!" – Master Hakuin roared outside Suatte's door.

At 11:59 Suatte got up and opened the door. When he did – he saw a big frown on his master's face.

"Why did you break your resolve?" – Master Hakuin asked angrily.

.   .   .   .   .

Mumon's comment:

For good or for bad we must stay earnest in our endeavors. Only then we shall achieve perfection!

But what if the monastery was on fire?

Zen Master – Suzuki Etsudo

An Interpretation

Sitting in Zazen is not easy. For a beginner, even a few minutes can be hard to bear. Most Westerners find it particularly difficult to sit in a lotus position (see the picture of Master Etsudo on the previous page). Their knees and ankles are not accustomed to it. For most Japanese sitting in a lotus position is relatively easy, because they spend much time on tatami mats since childhood.

The physical discomfort is not the only difficulty for a practitioner of Zazen. It is not easy to focus on breathing, to relax, and to completely forget about the external world. Hence, Zazen, similarly to martial arts, teaches self-discipline.

In this story, Master Hakuin tests his student's determination and concentration. In martial arts, the teacher also often checks the students' inner strength. The students adopt certain stances and the teacher tests their ability to resist kicks and punches and not to be thrown off balance. Unfortunately for Suatte, Master Hakuin manages to throw him off and to break his concentration. Ironically "suatte" means to "sit" in Japanese.

In his comment Mumon says: "For good or for bad we must stay earnest in our endeavors!" Doing our best will lead us to perfection, but of course we must be sensible about it. If the monastery had been on fire, Suatte should have responded to the alarm by escaping to safety. Perhaps then Suatte did not completely fail his test?

Ask yourself:

1. Are you good at keeping your resolve? Do you usually bring your projects to fruition? Do you ever make New Year's resolutions? If so, do you keep or fulfil them?

2. In many areas achieving perfection requires strong will and discipline. Do you have strong will? For example – have you ever successfully adhered to a diet or gave up a bad habit, such

as smoking or drinking alcohol? Have you ever persevered in a study program, body building, or some other long term, goal oriented activity?

3. Do you think that meditation can help in developing strong will or determination? If so, how?

4. What does the expression: "No pain – no gain!" mean to you? Does it apply to your life?

5. "Success without hard work is worthless!" – do you agree with this statement?

6. If all people could effortlessly become what they want – there would be no point in competing. What would the world be like without competition?

7. Do you want to be average or better than others? If the latter is the case – in what areas do you want to be better than average? For example – knowledge, bodily strength or endurance, will power, courage, intelligence, creativity, beauty, etc.

8. Is it selfish to try to outshine others? Can a person be better than others in humility, love and kindness? Is it selfish to try to be more virtuous than others?

Cherry Blossom

"Master Hakuin, let's go out to the park to see the beautiful sakura flowers!" – said Pretty Rose one day.

"Oh, Pretty Rose, please go there with other disciples, because I have lots of work to do." – responded Master Hakuin.

"But Master, don't you want to see the beautiful sakura flowers? They will be all gone in just a few days..." – insisted Pretty Rose.

"All beauty is fleeting – even that of Mount Fuji." – replied Master Hakuin.

Mumon's comment:

Is Mount Fuji as short-lived as cherry blossoms, or is Master Hakuin's life too short to see the difference?

Which beauty is less fleeting: the moon, the rain, the mountains, or the flowers?

An Interpretation

Two, most popular symbols of Japan are cherry blossoms and mount Fuji.

Sakura trees are cultivated in many parks and gardens, and people love to admire their beautiful blossoms.

Sakura trees bloom for a very short time – only one or two weeks in the spring, which comes to the different regions of Japan at slightly different times of the year. In Okinawa, where the climate is the hottest– sakura trees bloom in January, but in Tokyo and in most parts of Honshu Island – they bloom in the beginning of April. During that time, Hanabi Festivals ("Flower Festivals") are held across Japan and people celebrate by picnicking under the blooming trees. White or slightly pink sakura flowers look like snowflakes on trees, and just as snowflakes would do in a warm weather – they "melt" away very quickly.

Since the times of samurai, sakura blossoms were said to express the spirit of bushido or the samurai warrior – being vibrant and full of youthful energy, yet ready to instantly sacrifice one's life in defense of honor and the accepted values. During WWII the pictures of sakura flowers were painted on kamikaze airplanes and sakura twigs were taken by kamikaze pilots on their suicide missions.

While sakura flowers symbolize briefly passing beauty, Fuji Mountain is a symbol of stability, endurance, and longevity.

In this story, Pretty Rose feels alarmed by the brevity of beauty. Master Hakuin remains calm, because he recognizes the passing nature of all things. Life constantly changes its forms, and there is no reason to favor the beauty of those things which are briefer or rarer than others. Yet, this is the tendency of most human beings. Many people are very excited about the events (natural or manmade), which occur only briefly and sporadically – such as the unusual lining up of the planets, eclipses, rarely blooming flowers, etc. Similarly, rare materials and natural resources are thought to be precious and they are held in high esteem. Gold, silver, platinum, diamonds, and other precious stones are rare – and therefore highly valued.

Should we indeed value only that which is rare or brief? Or should we adopt Master Hakuin's attitude and value all beauty – even that which seems daily or mundane?

Ask yourself:

1. If gold was the most common metal on Earth, but steel was exceptionally rare – would you rather have a pendant of steel or of gold?

2. Do you prefer to wear unique clothes or mass-produced clothes? Do you wear jeans? Are jeans unique or mass-produced?

3. Artists like to be unique. Why do you think it is so?

4. Is it common or unique to value common things? Is Master Hakuin's philosophy common or unique?

5. Some people say that the average features are the most beautiful. A beautiful body is neither too small nor too large, but of an average size and shape. Do you agree with this definition of beauty?

6. Have you ever seen a handsome ant? Why do you think people can think of other people as handsome or ugly, but all ants seem alike? Similarly, if a person is not accustomed to seeing people of other races – it is hard for him or her to point out a handsome person of another race. For example, many Japanese women who are not used to seeing white men – cannot "correctly" identify a handsome Westerner! When I first came to Japan – all faces seemed similar to me. Why complete lack of familiarity makes us unable to identify beauty?

7. On the other hand, there is an expression which says: "Familiarity breeds contempt". Do you agree with it? Are

the people who make themselves scarce and mysterious, or "hard to get" more interesting than those who are easily encountered? If so, why?

8. If a man marries a beautiful woman (or vice-versa, a woman marries a handsome man) how soon does that person stop noticing and appreciating the beauty of his or her partner? Do you know of any such cases in real life? How fast does easily accessible beauty wear off for you?

9. Do you notice "the beauty" of your own health? Do you notice and appreciate it on daily basis? Why do we tend to appreciate health only when we have lost it?

10. How can we refresh our awareness and appreciation of the beauty that surrounds us in daily life (the beauty of the blue sky, the landscape, the sun, etc.?)

A mountain and a flower – both pass away quickly!

The Bumblebee of Enlightenment

Master Hakuin was sitting on the mountaintop surrounded by his two cats, seven dogs, nine chickens, and eleven rabbits.

"Master, please teach us about the Buddha-nature of the world!" – asked dog Inu.

"Very well!" – responded Master Hakuin. "The Buddha-nature of the world is..."

Suddenly a bumblebee interrupted his words flying by ferociously and noisily, so that all the animals dispersed in a hurry. The bumblebee made a few circles in the air and plunged into Master Hakuin's ear.

"A bumblebee in my ear!" – screamed Master Hakuin in panic.

At that moment the bumblebee was enlightened.

. . . . .

Mumon's comment:

All creatures are equally precious, even if some become enlightened sooner than others – just like all cherry blossoms are equally beautiful, even if some bloom sooner than others.

So light...

and enlightened!

An Interpretation

It is true that Master Hakuin had 2 cats, 7 dogs, 9 chickens, and 11 rabbits in his care. He also took care of a crow, a pigeon, and various other animals in the course of his life. Of course Master Hakuin was not Saint Francis of Assisi – who famously gave sermons to some fish and other creatures. Nonetheless, it can be said that Master Hakuin did speak to his animals. Anyone who has pets knows that talking to them is natural. On the other hand connecting with a bumblebee is pretty unusual.

The bumblebee interrupted Master Hakuin just as he was about to state what he thought about the Buddha-nature. The exclamation "a bumblebee in my ear!" became the answer and it supposedly enlightened the insect. Perhaps this unexpected statement enlightened Master Hakuin too. Indeed – the Buddha-nature is present in every creature, be it a fly or a ladybird – as implied by the pictures above.

Ask yourself:

1. Have you ever talked to any animals? If so, were you successful in communicating with them?

2. Just because we can't teach a human language to other animals (except for some words to parrots, monkeys, dogs, and pigs, and some hand gestures to dolphins), it doesn't mean that animals have no languages. It would be a mark of intelligence if humans could learn the languages of other animals – but for most of us it is impossible. Do you think that someday we will learn to speak with other animals?

3. Scientists learned that honey bees can show the way to the food they had discovered by "dancing" in front of other bees. Flying in the air in front of her sisters, a bee can inform them about the exact location of food. The dance of the bee may perhaps read like this: "You must go to the end of the forest, by the river, and on the left bank of the river near the bridge

you will find a sandwich dropped by some schoolchildren." It's quite amazing, isn't it? Do you believe that animals have their own languages? Do you know any "words" in dog language? What does tail wagging usually mean? What does bearing teeth usually mean?

4. In his book *Thus Spoke Zarathustra* Friedrich Nietzsche describes how Zarathustra speaks to and teaches his animals. The image of a human being communicating with animals has a strong appeal. Why do you think it is so?

5. Another famous literary character who can communicate with animals is Tarzan from the book by Edgar Rice Burroughs *Tarzan of the Apes*. Can you think of other famous characters in books and movies who can speak with animals?

6. There is a belief in the Christian lore that animals can speak in human tongues at midnight on Christmas Eve. Have you ever heard about this belief? Why do you think the magical ability to speak in human tongues would be granted to animals at that time?

7. Children often talk to their teddy bears and other animal toys, but they rarely talk to any inanimate objects such as bicycles or chairs. Why do you think it is so?

Obasute Yama

"Obasute" – in Japanese means "to abandon an old woman". Poor villagers of long ago, who lived at the foot of Mt. Obasute in Nagano prefecture are said to have left their elderly on the top of the mountain to die. For the economical relief of the family, the non-productive elderly had to be disposed of.

"But the elderly can teach the young ones about life!" – said Naidesu upon hearing about this from Master Hakuin. "I don't believe this story is true!" – she added.

"Are the modern retirement homes for the elderly not true? Are the people in those homes not life-wise?" – asked Master Hakuin.

.   .   .   .   .

Mumon's comment:

In times of peace – war seems unimaginable. Yet, the first act of war is disagreeing with another.

An Interpretation

The story of Obasute Yama is well known in Japan, but not everyone believes in its historical authenticity. Whether the residents of the nearby villages really left their elderly to die on the top of Mount Obasute, or if it was only a myth created by an artist – nonetheless the story had a great impact on the Japanese culture, and Obasute Yama has been mentioned in many works of art, including poems, short stories, novels, and movies.

Mount Obasute

The above photo was taken at the top of Obasute Yama. On the monument we read: "Obasute Yama no tsuki de kore." It means: "Mt. Obasute's moon is here." These words are taken from a well-known *tanka* poem, featured in the collection of Japanese folk tales – *Konjaku Monogatari, Yamato Monogatari*. Tanka poems consist of 5 lines (5, 7, 5, 7, 7 syllables), while haiku poems consist of 3 lines (5, 7, 5 syllables).

Waga kokoro	When I see the moon
Nagusame kanetsu	Shining in the sky
Sarashinaya	Over Mount Obasute
Obasute Yama ni	In Sarashina
Terutski wo mite.	My heart is filled with sadness.

Despite its fame, or infamy, not many people visit Mount Obasute. For me it was of particular interest, because of my own family history. In some sense, by visiting Mount Obasute I tried to say goodbye to my mother, whom I was not able to visit during her last days. Her passing away was unexpectedly quick and I didn't understand the urgency at that time. I still seek her forgiveness for not being by her side during those days.

Even if the practice of abandoning the elderly on top of a mountain is only a myth, all too often we abandon our parents or grandparents in the elderly homes, hospitals, or simply in their homes. Lonely and unattended, the elderly feel not needed and unwanted, and soon they lose their will to live. Just as the parents have a moral obligation to care for their children, the children have a moral obligation to care for their parents when they grow old. We should remember this in our very busy and very independent modern life.

An interesting illustration of the legend of Mt. Obasute and of the problem of abandoning the elderly is portrayed in the movie *Will to Live*, written and directed by Kaneto Shindo (who has also directed *Onibaba*), released in 1999. The movie talks about an elderly man who reads a book about Mt. Obasute and who is abandoned by his three children in an elderly home. Except for the final scene of killing crows and thereby unnecessarily promoting cruelty to these very clever birds, I found the movie thoughtful and informative.

Ask yourself:

1. Do you agree that children have a moral responsibility to care for their parents when they become old and infirm?

2. Do you take good care of your parents? Do they require any financial or emotional care? Do you have any siblings? If so, do they support your parents in any form?

3. Do you remember the movie *Grumpy Old Men*? Is it difficult to take care of senile, old people? If so, why?

4. Was the relationship between you and your parents good or bad when you were growing up? What were (or are) the vices and the virtues of your parents?

5. According to the Western lore, father and son often become rivals. This rivalry manifested in the son's desire to dethrone his father, is called *Oedipus complex*. (The term was coined by Sigmund Freud after the ancient Greek tragedy by Sophocles titled *Oedipus Rex*). Similarly, a growing up daughter may want to take the place of her mother and become the alpha female in the family. (This idea was proposed by Carl Gustav Jung and called *Electra complex*.) Have you ever noticed any rivalry between you and the parent of your gender? Do you think that the belief in Oedipus complex or Electra complex may have a negative impact on the attitude of the parents towards the same gender children?

6. What would the ideal parents be like? What is the role of a good parent?

7. If you are a parent – are you a good one? What are your strengths as a parent?

8. In the book titled *The Prophet* Kahlil Gibran writes: "Your children are not your children. (...) They come through you, but not from you. (...) You may give them your love, but not your thoughts, for they have their own thoughts. You may house their bodies, but not their souls, for their souls dwell in the house of tomorrow." Do you agree with this description of the role parents should play?

9. If the elderly people have no children of their own or if their children are not with them – who should take care of them and how? Have you ever taken care of an elderly person who was not your family member?

10. How can you interpret the following picture titled *The Path of Life*?

Zen Spear

A group of boys moved swiftly up the river. One of them had a spear in his hands. He bent over a nook in the rocks on the riverbed and thrust his spear in. When he pulled it out, there was a fish pierced through its side and helplessly wiggling on the end of the spear.

All boys cheered with admiration:

"Great catch! Good job!" – they shouted.

"I forgive you" – said the dying fish – "for I was a fisherman just like you in my last incarnation."

Mumon's comment:

Is this a Zen story? If you don't think so, you should give up your study of Zen and stick to fishing!

An Interpretation

This is a story about mindless and unnecessary killing of fish, who are, of course, our fellow creatures and our brothers and sisters. According to modern science fish are sentient beings, that is – they can feel pleasure and pain. According to Buddhism, fish participate in the process of reincarnation and should never be unnecessarily and intentionally harmed or killed. Personally, I like the famous words of Franz Kafka, who, after becoming a vegetarian, looked at the fish in an aquarium and said: "Now I can look at you in peace. I don't eat you anymore."

In Japan eating fish is extremely popular. Some of the forms of serving fish are particularly distasteful to me. *Sushi* is raw fish, but *sashimi* is fish eaten not only raw, but also alive. One of the most morally disagreeable "dishes" is *odori ebi* – a baby shrimp. It is served still alive and moving its legs and antennas while being eaten. True Zen cuisine rejects serving sentient beings as food – on moral grounds. It is bad to harm animals not only because of their suffering, but also because violence limits our compassion and prevents our hearts from reaching their full potential.

To those who say that predation is normal in nature – we may reply that there is a difference between the roots of a flower and its petals. While the roots grow in the dark soil and struggle to survive, the petals just bask in the sun and enjoy the blue sky. While the animals at the earlier stage of evolution must resort to bloodshed in order to survive, human beings don't need to harm other animals for sustenance and are much better off health-wise when they abstain from eating meat (and fish).

Mumon says that *Zen Spear* is a Zen story, because Buddhism often teaches us to be compassionate to all the creation. Siddhartha Gautama Buddha was a vegetarian and so were many Bodhisattvas. In one famous story Buddha wants to save a rabbit from being eaten by an eagle and offers the eagle his own arm as a meal (to be eaten instead of the rabbit). This kind of behavior is not a fantasy in Tibet.

When a Tibetan monk dies, his body is usually cut up into pieces and offered to the birds and other wild animals. Thus, the predatory animals that feed on human remains don't need to kill other animals that day! It is called *sky burial*.

In the Western tradition such famous figures in Catholicism as Saint Francis of Assisi, and in Orthodox Christianity as Saint Isaac the Syrian – were devoted to compassion and love for all beings. Saint Francis of Assisi was famous for preaching to the birds and fish. He is well-known as a *friend of all animals*. Saint Isaac the Syrian said: "What is a merciful heart? It is a heart on fire for the whole of creation: for humans, for birds, for animals, for demons, and for all that exists."

An American Zen teacher – Philip Kapleau – the author of *To Cherish All Life: A Buddhist Case for Becoming Vegetarian* quoted the Essene Gospel of Peace to illustrate that Jesus was a vegetarian.

Ask yourself:

1. Are you a staunch meat-eater or could you consider becoming a vegetarian if you were convinced that animals suffer in the process of being turned into meals?

2. Hitler was a vegetarian, yet he orchestrated the holocaust. How is it possible for a vegetarian to be so ruthless and cruel? Hitler was interested in vegetarianism only for his own physical health. Hitler was not interested in protection of animals. For what reasons besides health can a person choose to be a vegetarian?

3. Albert Einstein, who also was a vegetarian, said: "Nothing will benefit human health and increase the chances for survival of life on Earth as much as the transition to a vegetarian diet." Why could vegetarianism improve the chances for survival of life on Earth?

4. A Japanese writer Kenji Miyazawa was a vegetarian. His famous story titled *The Restaurant of Many Orders* talks about two hunters who get lost in the woods and find out what it feels like to become the prey. Do you know this story? Do you know any other literary stories or movies where humans are hunted as food?

5. If some aliens, who are technically superior to humans, ate the flesh of human beings, would you think of them as morally highly developed?

6. Albert Schweitzer was a famous doctor and a humanitarian. He was a vegetarian on compassionate grounds. When he lived in Africa he wrote that he felt sorry for moths and other insects that fall into the flames of candles. Thus Doctor Schweitzer chose to limit the use of candlelight in order to protect those insects. What do you think about his attitude towards insects?

7. Jainism is a religion in India which promotes the belief in reincarnation and compassion towards all beings. The believers wear masks on their faces in order to avoid accidental swallowing of insects. What do you think about such radical behavior? Is wearing masks a good way to "advertise" compassion?

8. When you drive a car and see a dog or a cat on the road – do you try to stop and avoid hitting the animal? What do you do when you see a small animal on the road such as a turtle or a frog?

9. George Bernard Shaw said: "Animals are my friends and I don't eat my friends." Are animals your friends? Many people eat meat because they don't make the connection between the packaged meat or a prepared meal (such as a hamburger) and killing an animal. Would you be able to kill an animal with your own hands? If you had to kill a cow with your own hands or eat only fruits and vegetables – what would be your choice?

Shojin Ryori

The above photo was taken at a *shojin ryori* restaurant. Shojin ryori are Buddhist restaurants located near Buddhist temples. *Shojin* means *the pursuit of enlightenment* and *ryori* means *cooking* or *cuisine*. Unfortunately only some Buddhist temples offer this exquisite cuisine, which is strictly vegetarian.

Except for rice, all the dishes in the above picture are made of bamboo shoots. You can see bamboo sushi (not fish!) – in the upper left; bamboo in tempura – in the upper middle; takenoko rice (rice with bamboo shoots) – in the upper right; bamboo soup – below the rice bowl; and various other bamboo dishes. All the dishes are very tasty and not too expensive. The food is served in bamboo cups, bowls, and on bamboo plates. Chopsticks and forks are also made of bamboo!

In some shojin ryori restaurants not only meat and fish are excluded, but also root vegetables are not served, in order to avoid killing those vegetables. Fruits, nuts, legumes, and the vegetables which fall off the vine (such as zucchinis or cucumbers) are used.

Watch out!

Ask yourself:

1. When you see the above picture do you identify with the frog or with the driver of the car? Who says: "watch out!" to whom – the driver to the frog, the frog to the driver, the frog to itself, the driver to him or herself, or God to everyone?

2. If you were a frog – what would you think of humans and their machines? Are human beings in general mindful of other species or blind and self-concerned?

3. In Chubu and Kanto regions in Japan people traditionally eat grasshoppers fried in soysauce and baby wasps in rice (the favorite dish of Emperor Hirohito). Have you ever eaten insects? If not, why not?

4. French cuisine considers frogs and snails (escargots) to be delicasies. Have you ever eaten such "delicacies"? If not, would you be able to bite a frog? What would be easier for you to do – to bite a frog or to kiss a frog? ☺

5. Frogs rarely turn into princes or princesses, but many "princes" and "princesses" eventually turn into frogs. Do you know of such cases? ☺

6. A famous Zen koan asks: "Does a dog have Buddha-nature?"

7. To understand it, one has to realize that in China (where this koan was first created), in South Korea, and in several other Asian counries people often deeply despise dogs and think of them of them as worse than demons. Hence this koan really asks if demons have Buddha-nature... Do frogs have Buddha-nature?

The Vow of Bodhisattva

"You should promise not to seek liberation until the last blade of grass is liberated!" – said Master Hakuin to his disciples.

"But how can I possibly enlighten the grass?" – asked Mondai.

"But how can I possibly enlighten you?" – asked Master Hakuin.

.   .   .   .   .

Mumon's comment:

The Vow of Bodhisattva is the vow of compassion. Promise to have a heart of gold – and you have found the path to Heaven.

An Interpretation

Bodhisattva is a person who is almost like Buddha and is about to become completely enlightened. After this incarnation Bodhisattvas may achieve liberation from the cycle of rebirths. However, being compassionate and knowing that this world is filled with suffering and ignorance – Bodhisattvas vow to return to this life on Earth to help other beings on their paths to enlightenment.

The vow of bodhisattvas is similar to Plato's vow of the king-philosophers. In Plato's book titled *The Republic* we read that the students of philosophy should vow to return to politics after having received their philosophical training. Plato believed that the most perfect and the most rewarding life was the intellectual life of a philosopher, whereas being a politician or a ruler required living in the practical realm. Yet the philosophers should accept their obligation to help others and thus they should govern countries or societies.

Noblesse oblige or *nobility obliges* – says the well-known expression. Perhaps all saints and wise men and women feel that they should help other beings, and that is why they engage in the practical life. It is true even in the Orthodox tradition where monks usually don't engage in missionary activities and don't try to improve the material state of the world (unlike Catholics, who feel obliged to feed the poor and care for the sick). The Orthodox saints make themselves available to the numerous pilgrims. They pray for the pilgrims and give them advice. When I visited Mount Athos, the holy land of the Greek Orthodox monks, I met a saint there – Elder Paisios (born Arsenios Enznepidis, 1924-1994) – who was busy with an unending lineup of pilgrims visiting his hermitage every single day.

The great East Indian thinker - Jiddu Krishnamurti, who was raised to become a spiritual leader of humanity and refused to accept this role, also gave his advice in the form of many lectures guiding his listeners to enlightenment.

Ask yourself:

1. Whom do you feel responsible for and why? As a parent do you feel responsible for your children? As a pet owner do you feel responsible for your pet? What do such responsibilities mean in terms of practical actions?

2. Should the rich feel responsible for the poor? If so, how? Is paying taxes a good way to support the underprivileged?

3. Should the wise feel responsible for the ignorant? If so, what should they do?

4. Socrates did not support the Athenian democracy, because he thought that common people without any special education could not rule well. Is the rule of the majority wise? Does modern democracy elect well-qualified rulers?

5. Do you want to change this world into a better place? How can it be done?

6. What does it mean to be compassionate? Are you a compassionate person?

7. "Might makes right" is the philosophical maxim supporting the Darwinian idea of the survival of the fittest. Do you agree with this maxim? If not, why not?

The Messengers of the Gods

Near Kasuga shrine and Todaiji temple in Nara there live hundreds of tamed deer. The deer are free to walk anywhere. At night they stick to the park area, but during the day they venture along the streets leading to the temple and beg for "deer cookies" – sold by the resolute vendors. A small pack of deer cookies costs 300 yen (about 3 dollars), which is a hefty price for a tiny bite. Nonetheless, many visitors to the temple are glad to pay it!

When Master Hakuin and his disciples visited Nara Park – they were approached by many deer. Master Hakuin spent all his pocket money – buying cookies and feeding the deer.

"Master!" – said Mondai – "These deer are constantly fed by all the tourists. Is it sensible for you to spend so much money feeding them, when you know that they will be fed by others anyway?"

"You are right!" – responded Master Hakuin – "I should have spent my money on beer instead!"

Mumon's comment:

The deer are the messengers of the Gods... as are cows, pigs, chickens, and all other living creatures. Are you ready to stop eating them?

The gate to Kasuga shrine in Nara

The Deer Park in Nara (Japan) is very reminiscent of the Deer Park in Sarnath (India). The Deer Park in Sarnath is where Gautama Siddhartha Buddha first taught the Dharma (the Buddhist teachings) and where the first Buddhist Sangha (the Buddhist community of the monks and the nuns) was established.

An Interpretation

The deer in Nara Park are so very cute! If a hunter visits the Deer Park and looks at the deer from up close, can he ever go hunting again?

Master Hakuin can't stop feeding the deer even though he knows that they are well fed by other people. Of course it is good to be charitable, but we can't help the whole world! We should choose the charities well!

When Mondai expresses his worries about Master Hakuin's choice of spending money, the latter ironically agrees and says that he should have spent this money on beer. Is buying beer the only alternative to feeding deer? Of course it is not! (Although the words *beer* and *deer* differ only by the mirror image of one letter – b|d ☺) There are many useful ways in which Master Hakuin can spend his money. He can donate it to Green Peace, support the development of rural Africa, or buy toys for orphans. He can also promote Zen Buddhism by giving this money to me! ☺

But instead, Master Hakuin simply follows his heart and acts upon his compassionate impulse to feed the deer.

It is unfortunate that with poor excuses we often stop ourselves from acting on compassionate impulses. We say: "Somebody else will do it!", "There are better ways to help others!", or: "They don't really need any help!", and we march on... often straight into a beer bar!

Ask yourself:

1. Are you a generous person? What have you given lately and to whom?

2. A wise aphorism says: "Whatever is not given – is lost." Do you agree with it?

3. What can you donate to others apart from money and material goods? Do you often spend time and energy helping others?

4. Do you think that life is a precious gift? Once you give a gift, you should never take it back. Yet life is a gift that seems to be taken back at the moment of death. When a person dies we say: "God giveth, and God taketh away." This implies that God takes back the gift of life. Is life a true gift, since we cannot keep it? Is life only a loan?

5. If your friend buys you an airplane ticket as a present, does it mean that after you use the ticket – the present is "taken back"? Life is a journey, and so, it is a gift that naturally comes to an end. If someone gives you a chocolate and you eat it – the chocolate is gone, but it wasn't taken back. God doesn't take life back just because it has an end. Do you agree?

6. Ancient Greeks believed that Gods could appear to humans in any form or shape. Sometimes Gods would disguise themselves as humans, and at other times as animals. If we adopt this belief – we should be very careful how we treat other beings. After all, they may be Gods in disguise! Are you usually gentle towards other beings? Is it good to think of other beings as Gods?

7. The Bible says that we are made in God's image. The main attributes of God are benevolence and justice. If God is good and just, and humans are made in His image – how should we act? What does it mean to you to be "good and just"?

Satori

"Master, what is the point of studying Zen?" – asked Mondai.

"To achieve satori (enlightenment)!" – replied Master Hakuin.

"And how can I achieve it?" – asked Mondai.

Master Hakuin looked outside the window. "Can you see that grassy hill?" – he asked. "Go to the top of the hill and sit down there in a lotus position, and think about satori."

Mondai did as he was told.

The following day Master Hakuin went up the hill to check on his disciple. When Master Hakuin got to the top – he saw Mondai busily plucking the grass. A large patch of grass has already been removed from the top of the hill.

"What are you doing?" – asked Master Hakuin.

"I am achieving ku-satori!" – answered Mondai.

("Kusatori" in Japanese means "to remove grass".)

.   .   .   .   .

Mumon's comment:

Mondai was a clever boy. In a room with only the tatami mats and a kotatsu table (Japanese low table) – the mind becomes clear of clutter.

Empty room – quiet mind

An Interpretation

Satori (*enlightenment*) and *kusatori* (*weeding out* or *plucking out grass*) are two, similar sounding words. The main part of the story is about the verbal misunderstanding and mixing of these two words. However, Mumon's comment offers an additional element to the story. Mumon tells us that removing grass is not as stupid or unrelated to enlightenment as it may seem at first glance. Why not? Because grass can be interpreted symbolically as scattered thoughts, worries, desires, etc. – filling out or overgrowing one's mind. Remember T.S. Eliot's poem titled *The Hollow Men*? "Headpiece filled with straw. Alas! Our dried voices, when we whisper together are quiet and meaningless as wind in dry grass..." In other words – grass may be interpreted as an unsettled mind, and as long as our mind is not calm, it is difficult or perhaps impossible to achieve enlightenment.

A traditional Japanese room has a very simple interior design. Tatami mats (or straw mats) cover the floor. There may be a small table in the room and a few pillows to sit on. There may be a haiku poem written as shodo – the art of calligraphy, hanging on the wall. There may be a vase with ikebana, standing in a special nook in the wall, built for that purpose. (The nook looks like a closet without a door and it is built especially for an ikebana vase and a shodo painting.) Such simplicity is meant to induce calmness of the mind.

In our Western dwellings we often surround ourselves with tons of furniture, trinkets, decorations, and gizmos of all sorts. We often expose ourselves to too much noise – from television, radio, internet, and street advertisements. Perhaps we should follow the example of the Japanese calm and tranquil households? Perhaps we should try to be more focused, like Zen practitioners?

Ask yourself:

1. Do you like to decorate your room with many trinkets? Do you have any paintings or posters on the walls? Do you like the Japanese style empty interior? If so, why do you like it? If not, why not?

2. Are you a tidy person? Is your room usually clean? Some people believe that mess is an expression of being creative. Do you think that creative people often have messy rooms? Are you a creative person?

3. The image of an *absent-minded professor* is that of an academician wearing two different socks, having some rips, tears, and dirty spots on his/her suit, being unfashionable, and having unkempt hair. An absent-minded professor is, of course, too busy in his/her mind to care for such trivial things as fashion or cleanliness. Do you personally know anyone like that? Did Albert Einstein fit this description? Do you know any fashionable or classy looking professors?

4. "Less is more" is a phrase used by the minimalists. Minimalism is a movement in Western art, inspired by the Japanese traditional design and architecture. Do you agree that less may be more? If so, how?

Mu – Nothingness

Since Master Hakuin's parents had already passed away, whenever Master Hakuin needed someone to consult with – he spoke with animals and asked them for guidance. One day he asked a cow if his teachings about the Buddha-nature of the world were indeed correct.

The cow answered: Moo! Mu! ("Mu" is a Japanese Zen term, which means "nothingness", "neither is nor isn't", or it can be interpreted as "the true reality".)

Mumon's comment:

The cow is my mother! How can I not see it drinking milk from her breast?!

An Interpretation

This story is very short indeed, but it has a vast body of cultural reference. In India, where Buddhism takes its origin, it is said that killing a cow is equal to killing a Brahmin (a high-caste priest). Hinduism, Jainism, Hare Krishna Movement, and to some extent Buddhism – regard cows as protected animals.

Why are cows sacred in India? In Hinduism it is believed that cows are the descendants of the divine, spiritual beings. If we look for a practical explanation: cows are extremely valuable animals. They don't require much care – they can roam freely and eat grass. Cows are very gentle, not hard to catch, and they don't escape from people. Many people in India drink cow's milk and eat dairy products: yogurts, cheese, butter, etc. In the rural parts of India cow's dry dung is commonly used as fuel (and burnt in stoves). Bulls are strong and easily controlled, thus they are used for plowing fields and pulling carts. In other words – cows and bulls are very useful to humans and easily managed.

Of course a nation has to be sensitive to the plight of animals to think of non-humans as family members and of cows in particular as the mothers of the nation. India has a long history of such sensitivity.

El Toru or Bull God was also worshipped in many ancient Near Eastern cultures. Ancient Egyptians worshipped a bull god – Apis, and ancient Israelites worshipped a golden calf. In the Hebrew culture, after Moses led his people out of Egypt, the image of god as a bull or a calf became synonymous with idolatry and was rejected by Judaism. Perhaps that is why in Christianity (which was born amidst Judaism) Satan is depicted as a creature with bull's horns, hooves, and a tail (resembling a bull).

In modern-day countries with monotheistic religious background (where Judaism, Christianity, or Islam permeated the culture) cows and other farm animals are not treated well. In most developed

Western countries food animals are raised in factory farms. Milk cows are artificially impregnated and when they give birth – the calves are removed from their mothers. Male calves are then usually raised for veal. They are kept in tiny crates, so that they don't move and their muscles remain pale in color. The male calves are slaughtered after four months. Female calves are raised to become milk cows.

The milk cows are usually impregnated twice in their lives and then also slaughtered, because their milk productivity goes down with age. Normally cows could live up to 20 years, but in factory farms they are slaughtered at less than half of their natural lifespan. They are never allowed to walk or run, to have families, or to enjoy normal lives as all animals in nature do...

Is milk a healthy food? The Physicians Committee for Responsible Medicine (an American organization established by medical doctors) claims that cow's milk is very unsuitable as food for humans. Factory farmed cows are given antibiotics and hormones, so their milk is particularly unhealthy, but also free range cow's milk is unsuitable for human consumption. The cow's milk protein is meant for calves to grow rapidly. A calf grows many kilograms a day, but a human baby doesn't, and of course neither does a human adult. Too much protein causes all kinds of diseases, including diabetes, cancer, and osteoporosis. How is it possible that osteoporosis, which is a disease of calcium deficiency, may come as a result of drinking milk? Doesn't milk contain calcium? Yes, it does! But when a person drinks a glass of milk (or eats dairy products) the milk protein causes uric acid to be released into the bones. The uric acid washes calcium out of the bones and within 4 hours from the time of consumption the consumer loses more calcium from the body than he/she had obtained from the milk. If you are a milk drinker your calcium balance is always negative – you lose more calcium than you gain. That is why in countries such as the USA and Holland – where milk consumption is the highest in the world – there is also the highest percentage of people suffering from osteoporosis.

Ice cream, cheese, and butter are well-known contributors of cholesterol – the main cause of heart attacks and strokes.

In summary – drinking milk is not a healthy choice and in countries where cows are not treated well it is also morally unacceptable.

Ask yourself:

1. Unlike lions, tigers, or crocodiles – cows and bulls are not dangerous animals. Of course they can hurt a human being in self-defense, but they are not natural born killers. What do you think about bull fights? Is it a noble spectacle?

2. Among famous artists – Hemingway and Picasso loved bull-fights. If a human being likes to watch an animal die in agony – is he or she worthy of being treated as a beacon for humanity? Can you think of such a person as a great artist?

3. On the other hand, perhaps one should separate the artist from his/her art and not judge the latter by the moral choices of the former? Knut Hamsun was a Nazi sympathizer, yet *The Hunger* is a true masterpiece. Martin Heidegger was a Nazi, yet his philosophy of phenomenology is studied and admired by many. If you discovered that a famous artist, for example a movie star, was a racist, fascist, sexist, or enjoyed cruelty to animals – would you still watch his or her movies? Why are some artists (such as writers) easily excused for their moral choices while others (such as actors) are not?

4. Do cows have feelings? Are they capable of maternal instincts? If yes, how do you think they feel when their babies are taken away from them? How would a human mother feel if her newborn baby was taken away from her? How does a baby feel when it has no mother? Are cows just milk-machines?

5. The word "mu" means "nothingness" in the Japanese Zen tradition. In English there is a famous play on the word "nowhere". If you separate "nowhere" into two words, it becomes "now here". Now here is nowhere! So, where are we now? Of course we can talk about our location by reference to something else. For example I am now about 500 kilometers away from Tokyo. Tokyo is located in Japan, which is east of the Korean Peninsula. The Korean Peninsula is east of China and so on. But where is the entire universe? What does it mean that existence is nothingness or that universe is nowhere?

6. Mumon – the original compiler and commentator of *The Gateless Gate* – the classical book of Buddhist koans – is said to have spent six years trying to understand *mu*. Mumon said that *mu* was "the gate to Zen", and that it didn't mean "*nothingness*" as opposed to "*existence*". So... ask yourself again about the meaning of *mu* and ... think about it for six years before you try to answer it!

7. On a lighter note: everyone likes the taste of ice cream. What substitutes for milk can ice cream be made of? Have you ever eaten soymilk ice cream or rice milk ice cream? If so, did you enjoy it? Have you ever eaten non-dairy cheese?

8. Do you recognize some of the faces in the picture below? Can you identify the representations of Picasso, General Franco, Hemingway, Hitler, and Esperanza Aguirre? (In 2013, when Esperanza Aguirre was the head of the local government in Madrid she elevated the status of bullfights to a protected national form of art.)

9. This painting is titled *The Champions*. What would be a suitable alternative title?

Zen – Not at all

Kaisho style.
Formal, most clear version
of calligraphy – preserving the
original Chinese characters.

禅　全然

Gyosho style.
Semi-formal version
of calligraphy.

禅　全然

Sousho style.
The most creative (free or poetic)
version of calligraphy –
used most often in hanging scrolls.

禅　全然

The above characters are: *Zen* and *Zenzen* (*Not at all*). They are painted by Mrs. Saeko Suzuki – a Japanese calligraphy teacher at the rank of *dojin* (the highest rank). Japanese calligraphy is closely connected with Zen Buddhism. To paint (or write) flawlessly one mustn't be indecisive or fearful. One must clear one's mind and achieve *mushin* or "a state of no mind". Calligraphy is often practiced by Zen monks.

Zen Morality

"Master, is it true that Zen is not concerned with morality?" – asked Mondai.

"If I beat you up instead of answering your question – will you continue to be my student?" – asked Master Hakuin.

.   .   .   .   .

Mumon's comment:

To take away one's actions means to take away one's life.

Seeking a respite in the shade a bird sits on a branch, and the tree joyfully welcomes it. Only fallen leaves are free of care.

Motherhood

An Interpretation

Sometimes we hear that Zen Buddhism is not concerned with moral issues. This opinion arises from the comparison of Zen with other religions, such as Christianity, or Islam. While many religions have a lot of moral dos and don'ts, Zen seems to be free of explicitly stated restrictions and requirements. To be a Zen practitioner you don't need to pray four times a day, eat only after sundown during Ramadan, or go to mass every Sunday. Zen is not fanatically pro-life, or against the use of anti-conception. Zen doesn't condemn gay relationships and other "sexual depravities". Zen doesn't even advocate helping the poor and the needy... Or does it?

Actually, it does! Zen practice is established within the context of two religions that influenced it and prompted its birth: Indian Buddhism and Japanese Shintoism. Both of these religions advocate compassion and kindness in interaction with others. Although Zen doesn't proclaim the Ten Commandments, yet various Zen stories illustrate that one should be a kind, helpful, caring, and compassionate human being.

On this planet – to live "beyond good and evil" is not a sensible advice. Every action has moral consequences, and we either participate in making this world a better place, or close our eyes to the evils of this world and thus partake in the perpetuation of evil. When you see a dog hit by a car and don't stop to help it, but instead you rush to a temple to meditate – you are indeed running away from enlightenment.

Ask yourself:

1. What do you usually do when you witness an act of violence – for example: a man hitting a woman, an adult beating a child, a human beating an animal, etc.?

2. Do you think that children or pets should ever be beaten? Is violence an effective didactic method?

3. Have you ever been beaten or physically hurt by your parents when you were a child? If so, do you recall the reason **why** you were hurt, or do you only remember the fact **that** you were hurt and **how** you were hurt?

4. Capital punishment has been abolished in most countries in the world (in 140 countries at the time of writing this book). Only in 58 countries the death penalty is still accepted as a form punishment. Why do you think countries such as Canada, Sweden, and Norway have no death penalty, yet they have low crime rate and they are said to be the safest and the best countries to live in?

5. "Every day this world is becoming a better place, and you have an opportunity to contribute to it." Do you agree with this statement?

6. "Ask not what your country can do for you, but what you can do for your country!" How do you interpret these words of J.F. Kennedy? Would these words remain true and poignant if we exchanged the word "*country*" to "*planet*"?

Zen Monkeys

Many wild Japanese snow monkeys live in Yoshinetsu National Park in Nagano Prefecture. They often spend time in Hell's Valley – full of hot springs and rising steam.

When Master Hakuin and his disciples came to Hell's Valley – Atama said: "Hell is not as black as they paint it!"

Kokoro said: "In fact it is often white, covered in snow and frozen over!"

Master Hakuin said:

"Black or white, hell or heaven – these words describe nothing. The only thing of importance is how Zen these monkeys are!"

. . . . .

Mumon's comment:

When you have a monkey mind restless with desire – in Hell's Valley you may learn to put out the fire!

Humans are indeed the most restless beings of all and it would do us good to spend some time in nature!

An Interpretation

In Zen Buddhism the expression "monkey mind" stands for restlessness. Of course the goal of Zen meditation is to calm the mind. However, the monkeys in Hell's Valley seem very calm and serene. Many tourists come to admire them in their natural environment. The monkeys are very well behaved and as long as the tourists don't pester the monkeys, the monkeys pose no danger to the tourists. Does the expression "monkey mind" correctly stand for restlessness, or should "human mind" stand for restlessness instead?

Atama says that "hell is not as black as they paint it", because Hell's Valley is a beautiful place indeed. Kokoro adds that in fact it is often white, because in the winter Hell's Valley is often covered by snow, and the monkeys spend much time inside the hot springs to combat the cold. It is interesting that Hell's Valley freezes over (except for the hot springs) every single year! "Atama" – means "head", and "kokoro" – means "heart" in Japanese, but it is not clear if the use of these words as names in this story is of any significance. In fact, the distinction between the heart and the head – or the emotions and the reason – is a very Western concept. For most Japanese thoughts and feelings originate in the head, while the spirit resides in one's stomach.

Ask yourself:

1. Do you have a "monkey mind"? Are you usually restless and impatient or calm and patient? Do you think patience is a good quality of character?

2. What situations in your life require most patience? Do your children, students, parents, friends, or colleagues often try your patience?

3. What activities (apart from meditation and sleeping) calm you down most effectively? Does taking a hot bath, listening to music, or drinking herbal tea – relax you?

4. Is stress often present in your life? Do you ever "take a deep breath and slowly exhale" or "hold your breath and count to ten" in order to calm down?

5. The best way to combat stress is to keep in mind that all our problems are ... super tiny! ☺ There are many, many stars (and planets) in the Universe and our planet is like a grain of sand among them. You and I are but microscopic specs of dust attached to the grain of sand called Earth... Does looking at the starry sky help you put things into perspective and relax about the problems you face?

6. It is said that if a woman smokes during her pregnancy her child is more likely to have a short attention span. Did your mother smoke when you were in her womb? Unfortunately my mom did! This is probably the reason why I like short Zen stories! ☺ Are you able to stick to one activity for a prolonged period of time? For example – can you read a book for more than an hour?

7. We live in the times of fast food, fast modes of transportation, busy work environments, fast action movies, and quickly ending relationships. Are you a fast paced person or can you take your time to enjoy your life more deeply?

Crying for the Thief

When Master Hakuin's motorbike was stolen, he became somewhat upset. Although Master's feelings were barely detectable, they brought about astonishment in his student – Honto.

"Master, you seem sad! Why is that?" – Honto asked. "You always teach us not to get attached to things, yet you seem to have been quite attached to your bike!" – he added.

"I am not sad for the bike. I am sad for the thief!" – answered Master Hakuin.

Mumon's comment:

He who steals – loses.

He who gives – gains.

Such is the law of karma.

An Interpretation

After a few days the police recovered the bike of Master Hakuin. It was broken and left somewhere in a ditch by the thief or the thieves. The police told Master Hakuin that his motorcycle had been most likely "borrowed" by a group of local bōsōzoku.

Bōsōzoku are the Japanese troublesome teenagers who form scooter gangs. Their scooters are very colourful and adorned with many lights. The boys ride their scooters with complete disregard for the traffic laws: going over the speed limits, racing on the city streets, not stopping on red lights, zigzagging and swerving from one side of the road to the other, riding with no helmets, etc. Bōsōzoku scooters are very noisy, so their revving engines stir commotion wherever they go.

Amazingly, the police are much happier stopping regular drivers for slightly exceeding the speed limits, rather than dealing with those really troublesome youths. Is it because the bōsōzoku are often connected with the local yakuza gangs (the Japanese mafia)? Or is it because the police officers don't want to deal with such recurring and hard to manage problems? In any case – I have lived in Japan for 7 years and I have seen many bōsōzoku groups on the streets. I have never seen any police officer stopping them. At the same time I got some demerit points and paid a couple of steep fines for driving above the speed limit – 55km/h and 58 km/h instead of 40km/h, on out of town straight roads, surrounded only by fields, with hardly any traffic... Wow! ☺

In the story, Master Hakuin feels sad for the thief of his bike. I think that it is not easy to get rid of one's animosity toward a thief, let alone feeling sorry for that person. Master Hakuin is indeed a "black belt" Zen master!

Ask yourself:

1. Do you ever get angry at other people? If so, on what occasions? Do you always feel that your anger is completely justified? Do you ever regret having "blown off the fuse"?

2. Do you try to control your anger? If so, how do you do it? Are you successful at it? What methods of anger management do you know?

3. Do you find that as you grow older you become mellower and less prone to aggression? Why do you think it is so?

4. Jesus forgave his executioners. He addressed God on behalf of His executioners, saying: "Forgive them Father for they don't know what they are doing!" Why do you think He said so?

5. "Perhaps all wrongdoing arises from ignorance. While the acts of crime cannot be tolerated, the ignorant wrongdoers should be disciplined without hatred. After all, they didn't know what they were doing". Do you agree with this approach to crime?

6. Zen Buddhism teaches non-attachment to material goods. Do you feel attached to your material possessions? Do you despair when you lose your money? If so, why?

7. Is it good to give things to others? If so, why?

Zen Obon (Zen Harvest)

"This is the true Zen spirit – to prepare for death at the autumn of one's life and to accept the scythe with one's head bent down with humility and calmness." – said Master Hakuin.

"Let me lead the way!" – softly whispered a sunflower.

Mumon's comment:

At the time of harvest let us rest and remember our past ancestors.

Sand-flowers

An Interpretation

Every being is a universe. In the picture above we can see the sun and the planets inside the sunflowers. Sunflowers owe their name to their resemblance to a bright, shining sun with a mane of sunrays. However, the picture is titled: *Sand-flowers*, not *Sunflowers*. Perhaps it is so, because the sunflowers are portrayed as growing on a sandy beach. Perhaps we can think of a connection between the grains of sand on a beach and the stars in the Universe. Scientists tell us that there are more stars in the Universe than all the grains of sand on all the beaches on Earth...

When we are about to leave this world prematurely – everything seems so very precious. We touch the ground and feel the sand or the soil between our fingers and feel moved by the miraculous nature of life. It is hard to leave life and most beings are not ready to die when they do. This is why we must respect life in all forms. All life is precious, even the life of plants, and so the time of harvest is filled with sadness and melancholy. Traditionally people used to harvest wheat or rice by cutting the straws with a scythe. Hence, a scythe became the symbol of death and was placed in the hands of the Grim Reaper. When the time of harvest comes to an end – we celebrate our own dead. As fall turns into winter all nature prepares to become passive. As the winter's snow covers the earth – death approaches. This is why in Asia white is the color of mourning.

Ask yourself:

1. There is a Latin saying: *Lux in tenebris lucet – Light shines in the darkness*. What does it mean? The saying comes from the Bible, where in the prologue to the Gospel of John we read that "Light shines in the darkness, but darkness cannot understand it." Jesus teaches people, but people cannot understand Him. The original saying emphasizes the fact that light and darkness are completely different in their nature. But this fact can also give us another insight. Light (such as a beacon) cannot be seen well in the daytime. Light (of a beacon)

can be clearly seen in darkness. We begin to see the value of life – when death appears. Similarly, we often don't appreciate being healthy – until we get sick. We don't appreciate enough our friendships, or romantic relationships – until they end. Do you appreciate life, health, friends, and all other good things before they end?

2. Mahatma Gandhi said: "Live as if you were to die tomorrow. Learn as if you were to live forever." How do you understand these words?

3. Most beings are scared of dying. How can we overcome this fear?

4. I believe that dying is similar to diving. When you are scared and your body is cramped up and twisted from fear – it will hurt when you hit the surface of water. But when you are fearless and you jump into the water with your hands and legs straightened and your head aiming for it – you will enter the water smoothly. Of course Zen is supposed to not only make life better, but also to make death easier. What else can prepare us for death and make us less afraid of it?

The River of Meditation

"What is the best posture for meditation? Is it the full-lotus?" – asked Suatte.

"Floating motionless in a warm, lazy river – is the best posture indeed!" – answered Master Hakuin.

.   .   .   .   .

Mumon's comment:

The best posture is no posture at all. The best meditation is when no one is meditating. Here is the best posture for meditation: only the warm, lazy river.

An Interpretation

For the beginners, meditating in a lotus position is usually not comfortable. One has to get used to the discomfort of sitting with crossed legs and a straight back until all the sensations of pain and strain completely disappear. Hence, Master Hakuin says that one should feel like "floating in a warm river". In the West, people often choose to meditate sitting on a chair or even simply lying down – in order to feel most comfortable. However, lying down often puts one to sleep and sleeping is not the usual aim of meditation.

The ideal state of mind that can be achieved through meditation is the mystical experience of being one with the world. In this state of mind not only the body "disappears" from one's focus, but so does the self, or the ego. In fact the ego undergoes a metamorphosis and becomes ALL THERE IS. The mystics think of it as uniting with God. In the Bible God says to Moses: "I AM WHO I AM", (or "I AM HE WHO IS"), which can be understood as I AM the Existence Itself. This is what one feels during the mystical experience. And this is why Mumon says that ideally the person who meditates disappears and there is only "the warm, lazy river" – or the existence itself.

Ask yourself:

1. Have you ever had the experience of feeling one with the world? If so, what did you learn from it? If not, what do you think you could learn from such an experience?

2. Do the sakura flowers that bloom on the same tree compete with one another? Do the leaves on the same branch hate each other? If all beings were aware that they are just different manifestations of only One Existence – what would happen to jealousy, envy, animosity, hatred, and other negative emotions? If you discovered that all living beings are YOU in other bodies – how would you treat the others?

3. In the Bible Jesus teaches: "Love your neighbour as yourself!" and "Do unto others as you would want others to do unto you!" Do you think that the mystical experience would reinforce these teachings?

4. In Zen literature serene mind is often compared to a calm lake, rather than to a flowing river. Yet Master Hakuin is talking about a river. Why do you think he does that? What ancient Greek philosopher comes to mind when the image of *a river* is used as a metaphor for *life*?

5. Have you ever met any saints? If so, what were they like? If you haven't met any saints personally, think of Gandhi, Buddha, Saint Francis of Assisi, Saint Isaac the Syrian, Mother Teresa, and so on. What do you know about their character traits?

6. Why do most people want to meet a saint? Could you be a saint? If not, what vices separate you from sainthood?

7. Deep meditation can invoke the experience of oneness with the world, but it is not the only way to experience connection with other beings. Cheering for an athlete or a team and participating in their joy of winning also allows one to emotionally merge with others. At what other moments in life do you emotionally unite with others?

Good Zen – Zen Good

One day Mondai asked Master Kotae: "What is good?"

Master Kotae answered: "Good Zen – zen good!"

Mondai couldn't understand this answer, but he said nothing. Later on Mondai asked Master Hakuin about the meaning of the strange answer.

Master Hakuin explained: "Master Kotae's English is poor. He says "zen" instead of "then". What he wanted to say is this: If you practice Zen diligently and become good at it, then you will naturally be good. "(Achieve) Good Zen – then (you will become) good!" "Good Zen – then good!""

.   .   .   .   .

Mumon's comment:

If Master Kotae's English had been better – he could have explained it like this:

Being good is like being God with an extra "o"!

An Interpretation

All major modern religions of the world claim that God is good. According to Judaism, Islam, Christianity, and Hinduism – God is good and by the same token – God cannot be bad. This is one of God's limitations. Although God is omnipotent and He (or She, or It) is said to have no limitations, yet in some sense God is limited. God cannot stop being God. God cannot become a mean or ignorant creature. God cannot become powerless. God cannot die. And so on. In other words, the attributes of God are constant and they cannot change. One of the attributes of God is benevolence – or being good. In fact, God is synonymous with goodness! Hence, Mumon makes a linguistic joke and says that the difference between "God" and "good" is just an "oh" or a "zero". There is "zero" difference between "God" and "good"! In the Western culture the idea that "God" and "the Good" are the same thing is quite popular ever since it has been mentioned by Plato in *The Republic*.

Although most Buddhist schools (including Zen Buddhism) don't speak of God, we can think of the Buddha-nature of the world as the Divine Nature, or the Divine Laws of the Universe. Hence, Master Kotae says that if you study Buddhism diligently and become a Bodhisattva – you will naturally be a good person. Have you ever heard of the Buddha or the Bodhisattvas going around and killing people or animals for fun? I bet you haven't! But you probably have heard of the Buddha and the Bodhisattvas helping others!... Yes, indeed, the road to liberation leads through compassion!

Ask yourself:

1. Which of the following statements about being morally good do you agree with?

    a. To be morally good is to try to get what I want. (An egoist. A bully.)

b. It is impossible to be morally good. We are all evil. (A nihilist. A pessimist.)

c. To be morally good is to make everyone happy. (A do-gooder. An optimist.)

d. To be morally good is to help as many people in need as I can. (A humanitarian.)

e. To be morally good is to try to change the world into a better place. (A visionary.)

f. To be morally good is to do what I think God wants me to do. (A missionary.)

g. To be morally good is to work for the good of the majority. (A utilitarian.)

h. To be morally good is to act in accordance with a maxim, which I wish to become a universal law. (A Kantian.)

i. (Make your own statement about being morally good.)

2. It is impossible to help everyone. On the other hand, it is easy to say: "I can't help everyone!" and help no one. What is the right balance between enjoying one's life and helping others? Should we spend 10 minutes a month helping others or should we do it for 8 hours a day?

3. In the Bible we are told that Jesus could heal the sick and even raise the dead. Why was he not a "full-time healer"? Why did he choose to be a spiritual teacher rather than just a doctor?

4. Do you believe that the world is gradually becoming better and better?

5. If you could change the world in any way you wish – how would you change it?

Knowing Not Knowing

"Master Hakuin, what is Zen?" – asked Mondai.

"I don't know!" – replied Master Hakuin.

"Aren't you a Zen master?" – asked Mondai.

"I don't know!" – replied Master Hakuin.

Mumon's comment:

Master Hakuin is Socrates – he knows that he doesn't know anything. He is a Zen Master indeed!

An Interpretation

Master Hakuin is like Socrates. Although Socrates taught his students about life's rights and wrongs, yet he claimed to know nothing. How is it possible to know nothing and at the same time to teach something (other than knowing nothing) to others? The epistemological scepticism (the belief that humans possess no real knowledge) can, in fact, be a good starting ground for building ethics (the system of values where rights and wrongs can be identified). Let's think about it for a moment:

Are you sure that this life is not a dream? Are you sure that all your experiences are "real"? It seems that all beings experience things differently. What may be exciting, enjoyable, interesting to one person – may be boring, uninteresting, or disappointing to another. How can we say that our experiences are real if they are not objective and they cannot be shared or confirmed by others?

Are you sure that today you are the same person as you were 20 years ago? Are you sure of your continuity? Everything changes. Everyone changes. Can you say that you know anyone deeply if they continuously evolve? Do you know what other people or animals feel or think?

Are you sure that tomorrow the sun will rise? Can an asteroid hit the Earth and destroy all life on it? Can God bring about the destruction of the Earth? Can the use of atomic weapons bring about the end of this planet? If life on this planet can cease to exist at any moment, can you be sure of any future at all?

Are you sure of the past? Is your memory good? Do you remember your birth? Do you remember your thoughts when you were just a year old? Do you remember your thoughts from one week ago? Do you know anything from before you were born? If other people tell you about the past – are you sure they are not mistaken or lying?

Socrates and Master Hakuin believed that the world cannot be known with certainty. Yet, they believed that human beings should try to make sense of the uncertain world. Humans should try to choose the best beliefs – the most probable or the most profitable beliefs. However, remembering that our beliefs are not certain ought to make us sensitive, tolerant, and open-minded. After all – we may be wrong and other people may be right.

Ask yourself:

1. Is there anything you can be certain of?

2. Descartes said: "I think therefore I exist!" What does it mean to think? Is there a difference between thinking, feeling, and experiencing something? Perhaps Descartes should have said: "I experience, therefore I exist." But what does it mean to exist? Have you ever experienced non-existence? Perhaps after death we still exist. Perhaps we always exist. Does the word "existence" have any meaning, if there is no other state? What is "I"? Perhaps all beings are interconnected and there is no separate "I", but only "we" or the "I of God"? Perhaps Descartes should have really said: "There are some experiences, therefore there is some consciousness." But it would have sounded pretty lame, wouldn't it? How do you understand Descartes's famous words? Do you accept them as a true statement? Do you exist?

3. Descartes is considered to be the father of Western analytical philosophy. But was he smart? Descartes thought that animals were machines. To check how they were built, he performed vivisection – he cut them open while they were still alive. Descartes performed vivisection on dogs, rabbits, and eels. When the tortured animals made agonizing noises – he simply cut their vocal cords... What made Descartes so callous and inhumane? If Descartes wasn't "sure" that animals were machines – perhaps he would have been more sensitive. Do you know of other examples of "certainty" leading to horrors?

4. What do you think of people who are certain about God and are willing to kill in God's name?

5. "The only thing that I can be sure of is my pleasure and my pain." Do you agree with this statement? If pain is real and easily reproducible – should we believe that others can feel it too? If so, should we want to inflict pain on others, or should we "do onto others as we would want others to do onto us"?

F. Bacon

Zen Western Form

"Your Zen stories have too many Western anecdotes and references." – said a Zen critic to Master Hakuin.

"You have read many Zen stories, but have you embraced any of them?" – responded Master Hakuin.

.   .   .

Mumon's comment:

"Don't be concerned with the form!" – This is one of the main teachings of Zen Buddhism.

Jack

In

The

Box

An Interpretation

Every second Sunday at 10 a.m. for the past few months Jehovah's Witnesses have been coming to the apartment building where my school is located. They are not very successful in proselyting their religion, but they sure are persistent. They go in pairs – a young attractive looking lady (to possibly engage the interest of the opposite gender would-be parishioners) and an older chaperon lady (for safety and perhaps to assist with knowledge on the subject). Both of them are Japanese, of course. They came to my door as well and were ready to teach me about Jesus in English. Although Christianity is really close to my heart I showed them my Zenzen Stories in progress and told them that I was a Buddhist!... What an interesting sight it was: two Japanese ladies promoting Christianity to a Westerner who claims to be a Buddhist!

Of course Buddhism, and especially Zen Buddhism, is becoming more and more popular in the West (and vice-versa, Christianity is winning the hearts and minds in the East). The world is becoming a global village and intermingling of all the religions is only natural.

In my opinion, Zen Buddhism offers similar teachings to mysticism. The main idea of mysticism is that all the beings in the world and all the elements of the world are interconnected and interrelated, and that we are all One. This idea was proposed by Pythagoras, Socrates, Plotinus, Master Eckhart, St. Francis of Assisi, and many other European philosophers, theologians, and religious leaders. In the Christian Orthodox Church the mystical philosophy is present in the writings of St. Isaac the Syrian and the Dessert Fathers. In Asia the proponents of mysticism include Gautama Siddhartha Buddha, Jiddu Krishnamurti, the Dalai Lama, Thich Nhat Hanh, and many others. Muslim proponents of mysticism include Rumi, Ibn Arabi and other Sufi teachers.

When Yamada Mumon was asked about the connection between Zen and compassion, he answered: "Sitting in Zazen I become nothing and everything becomes nothing. I and everything – melt together.

So when I see a flower – it is I. And when I see the moon – it is I. There is no greater love than this!"

Although Zen Buddhism owes much of its appeal to the distinctly Japanese folklore – yet the ideas behind the practice are universal and not bound by any culture. Hence, the comparison between Zen Buddhism, Christianity, and mysticism seems appropriate, and it can hopefully enhance our understanding of the universal values offered by Zen Buddhism.

Above all, this book is about Master Hakuin – who loved all cultures in the world!

Ask yourself:

1. Can you interpret the painting titled Jack-in-the-box? The vase is an ancient Greek urn, and the flower growing out of it has Jack's face... Well, his name could be Jack, as in *Jack of all trades, master of none*; or as in *You don't know Jack!* ☺

2. As the world is becoming a global village, more and more people feel that they are the citizens of the world, rather than the citizens of the countries where they were born. How do you feel about it? Are you a citizen of the world?

3. "The wells may look different in different parts of the world, but the water in them is basically the same – it's all H2O!" What does this statement say to you?

4. Hollywood production is probably the main reason why American culture became so well-known and popular in the world. Internet offers us a chance to "travel" globally and learn about many cultures. What do you think about the globalization of the world's cultures and beliefs?

Many Zen teachers see the connection between Buddhism and Christianity.

A prominent Zen master – Yamada Mumon (1900-1988) – the abbot of Shofuku-ji in Kobe, opened East West Spiritual Exchange between Catholicism and Buddhism, and assisted in opening many Zen centers in the West. He frequently quoted Jesus and the Bible to explain the teachings of Zen to the Westerners.

A well-known Catholic writer and mystic – Thomas Merton said: "The future for Christians is Zen and Christianity."

Hannya

"Is that a troll or a goblin hiding over there?" – asked Pretty Rose pointing under a small, wooden bridge in the forest.

"I think it may rather be a hannya!" (Japanese vampire-like, female monster) – said Master Hakuin in response.

"We are in Japan and I don't think that trolls or goblins live here." – he continued.

"Come on, Master Hakuin! Surely you don't believe in hannyas, do you?!" – asked Pretty Rose twisting her lips in a grimace of irony and contempt.

"Sure I do! I live with one!" – answered Master Hakuin.

Mumon's comment:

Master Hakuin should

apologize to Pretty Rose

for his inappropriate joke!

And Pretty Rose should

put down her knife!

Be good – everyone!

An Interpretation

Hannya is a Japanese monster originally created in plays of Noh Theater. The monster has a scary face with devilish horns and frightening, wide open eyes. The monster represents a woman who is obsessed with her love for a man and is consumed by jealousy and hatred. The woman is torn by her unhappy love and thus her monstrous image evokes mixed feelings of fear and pity.

In 1964 a hannya mask was used in a famous movie written and directed by Kaneto Shindo. The movie titled *The Hole – Onibaba* talks about two peasant women (an older woman and her daughter-in-law) who kill wounded samurai soldiers in order to sell their swords and armor. The women's gruesome routine is interrupted when a young man, who used to be their neighbor, returns from war and informs them that the son of the older woman (and the husband of the young woman) was killed. When the young man tries to win the heart of the young widow, the jealous mother-in-law becomes a hannya.

In the Zenzen story, it seems that Master Hakuin is teasing Pretty Rose who had noticed something worrisome under a bridge. By pointing out that trolls and goblins are culturally foreign to Japan, Master Hakuin hurts Pretty Rose's pride. In retaliation, Pretty Rose responds with anger and contempt. Master Hakuin then compares her to a hannya – a monster with confused feelings of love and hatred.

Mumon criticizes both parties – saying that Master Hakuin and Pretty Rose are both unnecessarily antagonizing each other.

Perhaps the point of this story is to show how easy it is to say something demeaning or belittling to others and how seemingly innocent comments can cause an avalanche of negativity. Perhaps the moral to the story is that on one hand we should avoid criticizing others and on the other hand we should grow thicker skin and learn not to be overly sensitive and easily affected by the criticism of others.

On a deeper level of interpretation, we may also try to understand the meaning of *hannya* in the Buddhist tradition. The Japanese word *hannya* means *wisdom* or *perfect wisdom* and it comes from the Buddhist Sanskrit word *prajna* (*pra-supreme, jna-knowledge*). It is unclear why hannya monster has such a noble name. Perhaps the original maker of hannya masks was a monk called Hannya-bo, or perhaps the original art studio that made the masks was called "Hannya". Another explanation states that The Perfect Wisdom Sutra (a Buddhist text recited like a prayer) was believed to be particularly effective against female demon monsters. In either case, since *hannya* means *perfect wisdom*, perhaps Master Hakuin simply complemented Pretty Rose?

Ask yourself:

1. Do you easily get hurt by other people's comments? Do you tend to be overly sensitive or impervious to criticism?

2. While ultimately Zen is supposed to lead us to Satori and Nirvana, in practical terms Zen is also concerned with forging a virtuous character. Is being critical of others a good or a bad quality?

3. Do you often criticize other people? Do you ever think of others as "stupid", "incompetent", "unreasonable", etc.? If so, on what occasions?

4. What are the ways to become less critical of others?

5. What are the ways to become less vulnerable to criticism of others?

6. What is the role of the parents in developing confidence in their children? If you are a parent, do you try to instil a sense of confidence in your child or children? If so, how do you do it?

7. "The only difference between a genius and an average person is the level of confidence they have." Do you agree with this statement?

8. "Trying not to hurt the feelings of other people is like walking through the field of flowers trying not to step on any of them." Do you agree with this statement? Do you often feel "clumsy" in social relations?

Hannya

Not a Question

"Master Hakuin, I am new to Zen." – Kodomo said. "Is Zen fast and exciting like Taiko drums, or slow and boring like Noh Theater?"

Master Hakuin answered: "Ta-da-dam-dam-dam-dam. (– imitating the sound of Taiko drums.) Yowoo! Yowoo! (– imitating the chorus in Noh Theater.)"

.   .   .   .   .

Mumon's comment:

Is taming a horse like making an origami decoration or like building a castle?

Where there is no question – there can be no answer!

An Interpretation

Noh Theater

Most arts in Japan are said to be heavily influenced by, or even originated from – Zen Buddhism. Most Japanese arts, such as calligraphy, tea ceremony, landscaping, archery, fencing, poetry, etc., were originally studied and practiced by the Japanese aristocracy. Zen, especially Rinzai Zen (with its difficult and demanding contemplation of koans), was also studied mostly by the aristocracy, and so the Rinzai Zen monasteries played a vital role in educating the sons of the noble families. Noh Theater plays were originally intended for the upper classes, while Kabuki Theater plays were offered to the less demanding and less sophisticated audiences of merchants and farmers.

In this Zenzen story a new Zen student whose name is Kodomo (which means "a child") asks Master Hakuin if Zen can be compared to a slow performance of Noh Theater, resembling meditation, or to a fast and exciting Taiko drums performance. Does Master Hakuin's strange answer imply that both forms of art are Zen? Or is Master Hakuin simply teasing his student demanding from him a greater intellectual effort? If you ask a silly question you get a silly answer! Both interpretations could be true...

Mumon's comment is also quite unclear. The term *taming a horse* in Buddhism has a special meaning, which has to do with controlling one's desires and calming the mind. Perhaps Mumon wants to point out that while all forms of art have their own individual forms, yet, many different artistic activities develop similar qualities of mind or character. In fact one can attempt to achieve a calm mind by folding origami papers or by designing and building castles. In the Rinzai Zen tradition working meditation is just as important and as potent in achieving inner peace as is the sitting meditation (*Zazen*).

Ask yourself:

1. What is your favorite art or creative activity? Why do you like it? What qualities of mind or character does it reflect and/or develop?

2. Some forms of art and some activities are more demanding and more developing than others. While playing gun shooting computer games may develop alertness and accuracy, it may also have a severely negative impact on the player's psyche (by associating images of violence with pleasure and success). Which arts, crafts and daily activities are the most beneficial to our spiritual and intellectual development? Do you often engage in such beneficial activities?

3. When I lived in Canada, I often went to the movies and occasionally to the opera, but when I lived in Europe, I saw many theatrical performances. I think theater is more popular in Europe than it is in North America. In Japan I went to see a Noh performance only once. It seems that young people in Japan rarely go to see a play in a theater. Do you often watch live theatrical performances? What is the difference in experiencing a live theatrical performance from watching a movie? Is a theatrical production more stimulating than a movie?

4. Do you dress differently when you go to the theater or to the opera from when you go to the movies? If so, why?

5. In Ancient Greece, amphitheater seats were chiseled in stone, and so the theater had great acoustics. In Syracuse, in Epidaurus, or in Argos – fifteen thousand spectators could hear the words of the actors echoing in the stones. However, the facial expressions of the actors were indistinguishable to the further away seated audience. This is why the Greeks developed masks that could express feelings and be seen from far away. The Japanese traditional theater also uses masks. With the advent of television the ability to zoom in on the face of the actor made masks unnecessary. Are facial expressions important to you in your daily life? Do you often use your facial expressions and bodily gestures to convey a message? Do you ever practice your facial expressions (in front of a mirror) or are you unaware of your grimaces?

6. Do you ever imitate famous actors or actresses? Are you a good "actor/actress" in life?

7. Is it important to be able to act well in real life? Do you think that politicians and other public figures often focus on their acting skills?

8. Good actors have the ability to express their feelings well. If a person has no ability to express his or her feelings well – he or she may be easily misunderstood and rejected by others. Human expressions are both – universal and local. Can you think of some universal expressions that all people have in common? (For example: everyone smiles to express happiness or joy.) Then, can you think of some local gestures or facial grimaces that only certain social groups, or certain nations have in common? (For example: Greeks lift up their eyebrows to say "no".)

Zen Patience

"I have studied Zen for forty five years and I still don't really understand it!" – complained Master Hakuin to Grandmaster Kame.

"You must learn to be patient!" – responded Grandmaster Kame. "Zen is not like fast food! French-fries, burgers, and cola – they all may be tasty, but they will poison your body!"

. . . . .

Mumon's comment:

After seventeen years in the underground darkness cicadas emerge on the surface to live a few days in the sunlight and die.

After ten thousand incarnations Buddha is born to teach others for just forty five years.

An Interpretation

Most Japanese people are indeed very patient. Once they embark on a path of learning a particular skill – they persevere for many, many years. Most Japanese are also humble about their progress. A person who has studied ikebana, calligraphy, or tea ceremony for a decade still often thinks of him/herself as a beginner!

In America, a year of studies of any sort often makes one an expert!☺ Most North Americans like fast food, fast cars, fast progress, fast access to information, fast service, fast action movies, fast talking, and a go-get attitude. (Though, I find that many Canadians are more on the "teatime and biscuits" – British phlegmatic side!☺)

This is not to say that the Japanese society is less frantic at getting ahead. In fact, the Japanese factories often push their workers beyond the limits that would be acceptable in the West. Nonetheless, it seems to me that patience is a common virtue in the Japanese society and impatience is quite common in the West.

For the Christian mystics patience has always been an important virtue. Saint Francis of Assisi is said to have had these three primary virtues: compassion, patience, and humility. The following saying is attributed to St. Francis of Assisi: "Where there is patience and humility there is neither anger nor vexation." An early Christian church father – St. Jerome, known for having translated the Hebrew Bible into Latin, is quoted as saying: "Haste is of the devil!"

Similarly, an Islamic scholar and teacher – Imam at-Tirmidhi is quoted as saying: "Calmness and patient deliberation are from Allah and haste is from Satan".

A Latin proverb says: "Festina lente!" – "Make haste slowly!"

Ask yourself:

1. In your opinion – is it good to be patient and deliberate? If so, why?

2. Personally, I admit to having a short attention span. It takes a lot of effort on my part to stick to one project until it is finished. For example, writing this book is taking far too long! I am often tempted to focus on a different project. Is it the devil who tries to boycott my effort of bringing Master Hakuin's stories to the readers?☺ Fortunately, my kind publisher often calls me and reminds me to finalize this book... Has the devil ever tried to prevent you from completing your projects? If so, who won – you or the devil?☺

3. In the above story, Master Hakuin has a conversation with Grandmaster Kame. "Kame" means "turtle" in Japanese and Grandmaster Kame likes being slow! In South Korea, I was told that a man who is in his twenties is like a dog (filled with vigor), a man in his thirties is like a lion (in social prime), a man in his forties is like a camel (carrying the family on his back), and a man in his fifties is like a snake (wise but sneaky). If you were to compare yourself to an animal, what animal would you be and why?

4. "While being patient is often good, we shouldn't be too patient with ignorance, imperfection, and evil!" Do you agree with this sentence? If so, what does it mean to you? How do you fight evil, ignorance and imperfection?

Stuffed with Money

"What is money good for?" – asked Mondai.

"It is good for filling up worldly people!" – answered Master Hakuin.

Mumon's comment:

When Jesus was asked about taxes, He picked up a coin and said: "Look at this coin! Whose image can you see here?" There was an image of the Roman emperor on the coin. Jesus said: "Give to the emperor what belongs to him – the money. And give to God what belongs to God – your prayers and your worship."

And whose images are printed on the modern day money? Those of the politicians, rulers, and other worldly people. Incomplete, worldly people need money, but Zen disciples need only a bit of daily rice!

An Interpretation

Mumon has said it all. There is nothing else to add, explain, or interpret. Instead of regurgitating what has already been said I offer this poem/song:

Life is Weird.

Life is weird and mysterious
But some people are damn serious
All they want from life is money
They are really very funny!

All they want in life is power
Want to have an ivory tower
Look at others from the sky
But life sees them eye to eye!

Life is weird, life is strange
But some people never change
Never learn and never grow
They just want to roll in dough.

We all smile, and sigh, and cry
We all try, then die – bye-bye.

If you take a lift or stairs
You won't live two hundred years
If you have just aches and scars
Or two hundred brand new cars

If you build a nest, a house
If you are man, a mouse
If you swim, or walk, or fly
We all have to say: "bye-bye".

So don't worry 'bout the dough
Cause we all have got to go

So don't worry 'bout your stash
There is more to life than cash!

It turns out that Richard Gere – the famous Hollywood actor – is a Buddhist! He says that although he was born and raised as a Christian, he prefers to be a Buddhist, because "Buddhism stresses self-reliance. In Buddhism one doesn't ask God for good fortune, and one doesn't pray to a deity, but instead, one must rely on oneself."

Well, Richard Gere is probably wrong when it comes to some forms of devotional Buddhism, such as Pure Land Buddhism, where the devotees worship Amitabha Buddha (or Amida Butsu) and turn to Him for protection. However, Richard Gere is probably right about such forms of Buddhism as Zen. Zen indeed seems to promote self-reliance. Richard Gere says that self-reliance is a very Western concept, and he gives an example of such thinking: "If you want to be a millionaire... or if you want to be a billionaire – you have to work for it!"...

I suppose that Richard Gere has worked hard to get his wish fulfilled. Of course he also has a personal charm, good looks, good acting skills, and undoubtedly some good luck! And so, Richard is probably rich!

I, on the other hand, am only a hundredaire. I mean – every month I earn a few hundred dollars and soon after I am down to zero! Since I am very fond of Buddhism (perhaps as much as Richard Gere), I will try to work harder, so that one day I can become a thousandaire!☺

Richard Gere also states that Buddhism teaches that there is no separation between the living beings and that we are all One. He says: "Buddhism teaches that your happiness is mine, so if you want something from me – just take it!" "But" – he adds resolutely – "I am not talking about **me** in any of this, because **I** am very far from this..."☺ In other words, don't call Richard Gere if you are in need of a financial sponsorship!☺

Ask yourself:

1. If you are reading this book – it is unlikely that you are a *worldly person* – as Master Hakuin and Mumon call materially oriented people. A worldly person or an *external person* is someone who is interested predominantly in the material world (like Madonna in her song *Material Girl*). Why do you think the *internal world* is also important?

2. A Zen triangle is an excellent figure because it is perfectly balanced. It doesn't roll like a circle. When we develop all three faculties – the body, the mind, and the spirit (the heart) – then we become firmly grounded and unshaken by the changing currents and winds. Do you try to develop all three faculties? If so, how?

3. Wisdom is like a treasure chest hidden inside your mind. Information can be found in the outside world, but wisdom can only be found inside a person. In order to find it – one has to close the doors to the outside world, at least for a while. Without contemplation there can be no illumination. Do you agree that meditation is extremely important? If so, do you meditate often? (Meditation doesn't mean only sitting in Zazen, or sitting in an armchair and thinking deeply about the meaning of life. Working meditation is often practiced in Zen monasteries! You can meditate and think deeply about life while washing the dishes or walking your dog!)

4. Which treasures are more valuable – precious stones and metals or precious thoughts and feelings?

5. If you were given a choice between having lots of money and very little free time or having some money (but not much) and a lot of free time – what would you choose and why?

The Food of Life

A Western philosopher asked: "Master Hakuin, which type of life is better:

One filled with passion, desires, and danger – like that of Icarus, who flew high up in the sky, but when his wings melted from the heat of the sun, he plummeted to his death in the ocean...

Or is it a life of temperance, self-control, and discipline (that's at times too mundane and perhaps even boring) – like that of Daedalus, who was safe and prudent, yet who had to witness his son's tragic death?"

Master Hakuin answered: "A mayfly lives only about twenty four hours. A turtle may live one hundred and fifty years. But whose life is more valuable?"

.   .   .   .   .

Mumon's comment:

A theoretical comparison of different lifestyles is like a debate about different tastes of food.

Don't talk – just eat!

An Interpretation

Usually, children go to school, because it is obligatory. After elementary school most children continue to study because their parents told them to do so. During their high school years they don't know what they will do after. Then they choose a college, a university, a vocational training, or they go to work – but they still don't know what they are doing. They just find some opportunities and by chance choose their future. After joining some company, they continue working there until they finally retire. Sometimes they are forced to change their job, but it is not their choosing, it is not their passion that leads them. Most people don't follow their passions in their choices in life. They meet somebody on the basis of chance and they marry that person. They have children because it "happens so". They take care of the children in the same way in which they were raised. They don't assess the values they instill in their children. They don't try to improve on the values that they have inherited. They just keep the same. This kind of conformist behavior is considered normal, and being outside of it – behaving differently – is considered abnormal or mad. Any non-conformist behavior is regarded by most people as craziness.

To me, it is the other way around. It is crazy to be a conformist! It is crazy to follow what everyone does, without evaluating life from the beginning. Looking at life and being ALIVE – being here in this exciting and glorious world, filled with magic and beauty, but also with cruelty, surprise, shock, and disappointment; the world, which is filled with passion, desires, and hopes, but also with suffering, pain, and agony; the world full of life – is fascinating to me! And to live in it as if one had covers on both sides of the eyes and couldn't see to the sides – is madness.

So how can you avoid this madness? You should try to find the right way for yourself. You should try to find passion, because this is what life is all about. Having passion and experiencing life to the fullest are the key elements of being truly alive!

Imagine you are in a movie. What part would you like to have in this movie? Would you like to be a cameo? Would you like to be someone not important, who is just in the background of the action? Would you like to be a person who doesn't do anything special? Or would you prefer to be a hero? If you would like to be a hero, then try to be the hero of your life! Don't hesitate! Do something to be the hero!

Don't be afraid of trying, even if others look at you funny; even if others think you are not normal. So what?! What does their opinion matter? It is just some noise and commotion around you. What you are interested in is the real value of life and you know that there are but a few winners in this game. There are very few people who understand what life is all about. You can ask around: "Do you know what life is about? Do you know where we are going after this life? Do you know where we come from before this life? Do you know how to be happy? Are YOU happy?" Most people have no answer to any of these questions. So you have to rely on yourself. Evaluate life and choose what you think is best!

I often travel in this world. From time to time I change the place and go to a different country. I abandon everything behind me and move on in search of the right way, and in search of new experiences. I think it is very important to find new experiences in life, because they give you the ability to compare values.

HEART

OR

MIND?

Ask yourself:

1. What do you usually follow in life – your heart or your mind?

2. Interestingly, the Japanese don't associate the heart with feeling and the mind with thinking. Traditionally in Japan, thinking and feeling originate in the mind, and courage dwells in the stomach. When Japanese people point to themselves – they point to the forehead. When Western people point to themselves – they point to the chest. Where does your spirit reside?☺

3. Which periods in European culture and literature do you prefer: the "heart oriented" periods of flexibility, sensitivity and synthesis – The Antiquity, Renaissance, Romanticism, and The New Age (still coming), or "the mind oriented" periods of rigidity, calculation, and analysis – The Middle Ages, Enlightenment, The Industrial Revolution, and Modernism? Explain your choices.

No Gold for a Golden Heart

A poor man asked: "Is life without riches worth living?"

Master Hakuin asked: "Is life without cancer worth living?"

.   .   .   .   .

Mumon's comment:

Why does the Bible say: "It is easier for a camel to pass through the eye of a needle than for a rich man to pass through the Gate of Heaven"? Perhaps because in order to enter Heaven one needs to be compassionate. When 20 million people die of hunger each year – a compassionate rich person would very quickly give the wealth away and stop being rich.

An Interpretation

Gautama Siddhartha Buddha was once a prince, who enjoyed his great material wealth, but he gave it all up and chose to live like a beggar. Similarly, Saint Francis of Assisi had access to a financial wealth as a boy, because his father was a wealthy salesman. When Francis decided to follow Christ – he gave up all his private belongings and chose to live penniless. Why did these two, as well as many other spiritual teachers, choose the life of material poverty? They gave up their riches, because the material wealth is in direct opposition to the spiritual wealth. A person cannot serve two masters – God and mammon (spiritual and material wealth), says the Bible (Matthew 6:24). It is hard to be an owner of a few luxury mansions, a couple of airplanes, and some 200 Cadillacs (even if one gives away many of them as presents), and to claim sainthood at the same time! This is why Elvis Presley was not called a saint, but a king!☺ Kings often have great power and much money, but saints are the ones who "walk with God".

When you give up your material wealth and shut yourself away from the earthly matters – at first you will be surrounded by darkness. Slowly your eyes will get used to the darkness and you will begin to see. You will notice that you are in a dark cave of your existence. After a while you will notice huge trunks and grand sacks leaning against the walls of the cavern. When you open them – you will find that they are filled with treasure – gold coins and bars, precious stones, and fine jewelry. Of course the treasure is made of pure light. The jewels and the gold – are made of pure spirit. They are spiritual treasures – pearls and diamonds of wisdom, gold coins and bars of compassion, and the necklaces, rings, bracelets, and crowns to adorn the spiritual leaders and rulers. Wear them with... humbleness!

Ask yourself:

1. Is it better to be a rich fool or a poor wise person? Of course it's not a fair question. Bill Gates is pretty smart, right?☺

2. If there is such a thing as karma and every person gets rewarded for good deeds and punished for bad deeds in afterlife – who do you think would get a better judgment – Cleopatra or Mother Teresa? If karma is real – whom would you rather be – Cleopatra or Mother Teresa?

3. Which is better – to have a golden chain or a golden heart?☺

4. Poor people are often more generous than rich people. Why do you think it is so?

5. Having said that rich people may have a difficult time nursing and developing their spirituality, I want to say that some well-to-do people have been known to be extremely generous and goodhearted. I applaud and admire generosity of some wealthy people I have personally met. Have you met any wealthy and kindhearted people?

6. "The ability to make money may be admirable, but making money should not be our goal in life." Do you agree with this statement? If so, what should be our goal in life?

7. "Money doesn't buy happiness." – do you agree or disagree with this statement?

A Fallen Tree Trunk

"How should a Zen practitioner regard a tree trunk fallen across the road?" – asked Mondai.

"As a gate!" – answered Master Hakuin.

.   .   .   .   .

Mumon's comment:

Disappointed with the lax moral standards of the Catholic Church of his time – Martin Luther established his own school of Christian thought.

Difficulties and obstacles often inspire new solutions.

An Interpretation

Most people dislike problems and difficulties they encounter in life. Most people want to stay unopposed and be able to do what they want. Although we can certainly enjoy "smooth sailing" in life, we should also learn to appreciate the difficulties we experience. Without them we would never be able to "rise to the challenge" and grow. Without the hardships we would never become better people – tougher, smarter, and better able to cope with the environment.

Of course in theory we may all know that difficulties and hardships make us evolve, but it is hard to feel blessed and be thankful when we actually go through some crises. It takes a spiritual mastership to think of unpleasant experiences as blessings. In the *Book of Divine Consolations* Meister Eckhart (a Christian German monk and mystic who lived in 12th century Europe) gives us very concrete examples of this correct mental attitude. "If you lose one thousand marks (German currency) don't cry for the money. Instead thank God that you received an opportunity to exercise your virtue".

It is certainly much easier to cope with a loss of some material possessions than with a loss of a person who was important and close to us. But even then Meister Eckhart tells us to remain positive. According to Eckhart (and many other spiritual masters of various faiths) – death is not the end of everything, but a door to another reality. Furthermore, death is the end of mortal imperfection (at least temporarily, if we are to believe in reincarnation). "A loss of life as a creature is a loss of imperfection", says Eckhart in *The Book of Divine Consolations*, "and a loss of imperfection should not upset a good person".

Zen Buddhism also teaches us that much of our happiness and unhappiness depends on the mental attitude towards whatever we experience at a given moment. If we learn to think of the obstacles as beneficial – it will lessen our suffering and make us more resilient.

Personally, I find that often what seems to be a loss at first glance turns out to be a blessing. When I was fired from my first steady job (as a waiter in Beacon Arms Hotel in Ottawa, Canada) I actually remember that a single tear rolled down my cheek. "I had worked so hard and I had tried to do my best – so why was I being fired?" – I thought at the time and I felt deeply wounded. I was only 20 years old then and I didn't know how to cope with a loss of a job. A few years later I read Meister Eckhart's books and some teachings of Zen masters too – and my attitude has changed. When I was fired quite recently from a job as a teacher (because I had shaved my hair like a Buddhist monk and because I drank coffee in the classroom) – I literally laughed. It was a 180 degrees change in my attitude and thus a completely different experience. When I read the letter of termination of my employment (unjust as it might have been), I felt that God simply wanted me to do some other things. I felt free and excited about the unknown future... Perhaps I wouldn't have had the time to write this book if I had stayed on the job as a full-time school teacher.

Ask yourself:

1. Do you usually think of hardships as beneficial challenges? Do you ever feel thankful for hard times in life?

2. How do you usually deal with stress caused by life crisis? Do you eat a lot of chocolate or ice-cream, talk with your friends about the hardships you experience, drink alcohol, watch comedies, read good books, take hot baths, or do something else?

3. According to Aristotle, wisdom is "the ability to function properly as a human being". It sounds pretty vague, but it means that wisdom is the ability to live a prosperous and fulfilling life. If we accept this definition, we could think of wisdom (at least partially) as "the ability to solve problems". A wise person, a guru – teaches others and helps them find happiness. He or she finds the best possible solutions to their problems. Do you agree with this definition of wisdom? Is the

ability to solve problems a mark of wisdom? Does solving and overcoming problems in life make you wiser?

4. "The fire of suffering burns out all our weaknesses and earthly impurities and leaves only the diamonds of the resilient spirit to be found in the ashes." Do you remember *The Lord of the Rings* by J.R.R. Tolkien? What made the wizard Gandalf the Grey become Gandalf the White?

5. Do you agree with the well-known expression, originally coined by Nietzsche in his book *Twilight of the Idols*: "Whatever doesn't kill me – makes me stronger"? Do you often say it to yourself when you experience hardships in life? Do you ever console others in this way? What are other consolations do you use when your friends go through tough times? (For example: "Don't worry! Everything passes, so your problems will pass too!")

6. Does looking at the stars and remembering how vast the universe is and how tiny our planet is – help you cope with hardships in life? Do you think that the hardships faced by microorganisms are important?☺ (But maybe they are important – to them!)

7. Young people tend to perceive their hardships with great sensitivity. At times they even choose to kill themselves over such trivial problems as low grades at school. What would you say to such people?

Zen-man's Job

"Should a Zen-man have a job?" – asked Mondai.

"Does a Zen-man want to eat?" – asked Master Hakuin.

Mumon's comment:

Instead of hunting and gathering – modern man works. Eight hours a day of toil make your back stronger and your mind clearer during the practice of Zazen.

An Interpretation

In Zen monasteries monks often engage in physical labor – such as cleaning the monastery, cooking, or planting and harvesting rice. "No work for a day – no food for a day!" states one of the Zen monastic mottos. In Rinzai Zen monasteries in Japan, finding enlightenment through one's labor (samu) is considered more important and more effective than finding enlightenment through a seated meditation (zazen).

The Japanese society in general is very work oriented. Japanese people work usually longer hours (often without any additional compensation) than their North-American or European counterparts. While in the West people often tell each other "not to work too hard" and to "take it easy", in Japan people advise each other to "do their best at work". "Gambatte, kudasai!" – "Do your best, please!" is commonly heard in Japan. Wives say it to their husbands every morning, when the latter are leaving homes for work. In the companies, workers usually encourage one another in the same manner. After a day of hard work, Japanese workers congratulate and thank each other for the work well done. "Ockare samadeshita!" – "Thank you for having worked so hard!" is a common saying exchanged by all workers regardless of their position in the company.

When practicing martial arts and during Zazen meditation – the practitioners are taught discipline and endurance. Similarly, in Japanese companies endurance is a very important and highly valued quality. Even when the Japanese workers are asked to put in extra-long overtime hours – it is very rare to hear them refuse or complain.

Ask yourself

1. Do you know any proverbs or maxims expressing the benefits of being a hard worker or not being lazy?

2. There is a Yiddish proverb: "Work is no shame." There is a similar African proverb from Ghana: "It is no shame at all to

work for money." However, we are not best suited for all type of work. What type of work are you best suited for? Are you well suited for your present job? If not, what prevents you from getting the job you are best suited for?

3. Confucius said: "Choose a job you love and you will never have to work a day in your life." Do you love your present job? If not, what job would you love to have? What prevents you from getting this job? (You are likely to answer: "Reality!" or "Lack of opportunity!" etc., but remember that this question is not meant to be answered lightly, but to be pondered upon!)

4. Samuel Butler – 17th century British poet and satirist wrote: "Every man's (creative) work, whether it be literature, or music, or pictures, or architecture, or anything else – is always a portrait of himself." Do you agree? Is your spirit and personality reflected in what you create? Is Master Hakuin's spirit reflected in this book?☺

5. Products made in Japan are usually reliable and of high quality. What qualities of character are reflected in good workmanship?

Freedom or Responsibility

When Shijin met Matsuo Basho, the latter asked: "Wouldn't it be better to travel the world unhindered and unobstructed by the animals in your care, so that you could investigate life in the lands near and far?"

Shijin answered: "It is better to have three dogs in one hand and four in the other, than to have the whole wide world in your palm and be of use to no one!"

.   .   .   .   .

Mumon's comment:

Shijin was useful to his dogs, but Basho was a great poet, who needed to travel in order to create his masterpieces.

A river is flowing, a mountain is growing – thank God for both of them!

An Interpretation

Although freedom to do what one wants is an illusion, yet, the feeling of being a globetrotter is a very pleasant one! Most people long to be able to travel around the world in order to discover exotic lands and cultures, to see exotic animals and plants, and to meet exotic and interesting people.

When I was young, my imagination was fired up by the voyages of literary globetrotters, such as Sindbad the Sailor, the Little Prince, Gulliver, Phileas Fogg and Passepartout (*Around the World in Eighty Days*), and Odysseus. Even the musical albums of Vangelis – *China*, and of Vollenweider – *White Winds* – made me dream of traveling to faraway places.

I managed to realize my dream, and so far I have lived on three continents (Asia, Europe, and North America), in seven countries, for a few years in each one of them. However, with age comes the sense of responsibility. While travelling around the world, I started to help various domestic and wild animals, and I feel obliged to keep helping them. This obligation makes me less free to travel. It is hard to relocate with two cats, seven dogs, and nine chickens that are presently in my care! Being a parent of human children or of non-human children (pets) – makes it difficult to move around.

Ask yourself:

1. Do you like travelling? If so, why?

2. Do you think that the life of a globetrotter is more interesting than the life of someone who never relocates? If so, why do you think so? Are you a globetrotter? If not, why not?

3. Every physical adventure has a spiritual dimension. When we discover new lands and cultures – we also grow spiritually. But our spiritual growth can also take place independently of our physical location. When we read books and/or meditate – we

embark on spiritual adventures and broaden our minds and hearts. Do you often travel in your mind? What "worlds" do you like to visit in your mind? What questions and problems do you often think about?

4. Whom do you feel responsible for? Do you have a strong sense of responsibility? Has your sense of responsibility changed over the years?

5. "The more compassion we have in our hearts – the more we feel responsible for others. A truly good person can never abandon his or her dependents." Do you agree with this statement?

6. In the Bible (Deuteronomy 31:6), we read: "Be strong and courageous. (...) because God will not abandon you." Sometimes in the rain, many small animals (such as frogs and earthworms) come out on the roads and get squashed by passing by cars. Those days I try to collect the little critters from the roads and place them on safe grounds. When I do that, I repeat the phrase: "He will not abandon you!" and I feel at that time that my body becomes the vessel of God's will. Do you ever feel that you are doing God's will?

Zen Triangle

"Master Hakuin, why did you choose a triangle as your symbol of Zen?" – asked Mondai.

Master Hakuin explained:

"In Christianity number 3 represents the Holy Trinity: the Father, the Son, and the Holy Spirit.

In Ancient Greece number 3 represented: the mind, the body, and the spirit – which was expressed in 3 structures built next to one another: a theater, a stadium, and a temple.

There is the Artistic Trinity: the Author, the Audience, and the Artwork.

There is the Buddhist Trinity known as the Three Treasures: the Buddha, the Sangha (the Community of monks and nuns), and the Dharma (the Teachings).

There is the Temporal Trinity: Past, Future, and Present.

There is the Existential Trinity: Subject, Object, and Experience.

And finally, when you meditate in Zazen you look like a triangle."

.   .   .   .   .

Mumon's comment:

Furthermore, the name **Edward** starts with the letter **E**, which is the mirror image of *3*. Edward's father was named *Edward* and his grandfather was also named *Edward*, hence **this** Edward is *Edward* *the 3rd*. Finally, if you sum up all the numbers in Edward's birthday – it will be 3. It's just basic numerology.

Wait a second... Who is Edward?

An Interpretation

Master Hakuin's explanation why he chose a triangle as the symbol of Zen is quite clear. On the other hand, Mumon's comment is rather confusing. Who is Edward that Mumon is talking about? Perhaps King Edward III – the medieval king of England, who was the son of King Edward II and the grandson of King Edward I. However, King Edward III was born on November 13th, 1312, and if we add up all the numbers in his birthday the sum is 4, not 3. 11(November) +13(day) +1312(year) =1336=1+3+3+6=13=1+3=4. Mumon says that the sum of all the numbers in Edward's birthday is 3. Perhaps then he has a different Edward in mind...

Ask yourself:

1. What is the sum of all the numbers in your date of birth? Can you interpret the meaning of this number? If not, here is a quick guide to birthdate numerology:

   Number 1 – this person is very smart and rational. He or she can be a great leader.

   Number 2 – this person is emotional, sensitive and caring. He or she has good intuition. He or she prefers to follow rather than to lead.

   Number 3 – this person is very spiritual and can be a good spiritual guide or guru.

   Number 4 – this person is a good judge of character. He or she is fair and honest. He or she would make a good judge in the court of law.

   Number 5 – this person is very loving. This person follows his or her heart and also likes traveling.

   Number 6 – this person lives to the fullest. In the Bible, Jesus changes 6 jars of water into wine, because number 6 means

LIFE. Jesus symbolically changes average life (water) into special life (wine). The person with this birthdate number will get to understand the meaning of life.

Number 7 – this person has some cosmic purpose – a special mission in life. If this is your number – try to discover what you are supposed to do. Maybe you are going to find a miraculous cure for a serious disease or write a ground shaking book?

Number 8 – this person is going to grow and evolve in his or her life. This person will have many eye-opening experiences. If 8 is your number – you are a good learner.

Number 9 – this person is going to be successful in any undertaking of his or her choosing. You can do well in any business – so choose what makes you most happy!

2. Pythagoras was an ancient Greek mathematician who liked numerology. He was a vegetarian! Music was also very important to him. Do you like music? Is there a connection between music and numbers?

3. Do you believe in numerology? Do you have a lucky number? What numbers are significant in your culture and why? In Japan, number 4 is thought to be unlucky, because it is pronounced as "shi", which also means "death". How do you feel about number 13?

4. My father used to say that "mathematics is the queen of sciences". Well, he just repeated the words of a German mathematician – Carl F. Gauss.☺ Do you agree?

Keeping Promises

Master Hakuin was famous not only in Japan, but also in many other countries all over the world. Many Zen practitioners from foreign lands came to study with Master Hakuin.

One day, a foreign journalist who worked for a prestigious magazine was supposed to interview Master Hakuin. Yet, at the last minute he cancelled the appointment and rescheduled it for the following week. A few days prior to the scheduled meeting he cancelled it again. Finally, three weeks later he came to interview Master Hakuin, but he was late. Naturally, he apologized to Master Hakuin.

"Do you like Japan?" – Master Hakuin asked the journalist.

"Yes, I do! I like Japan very much!" – answered the journalist.

"What do you like about it?" – inquired Master Hakuin.

"Oh, so many things! I like the kindness of the people, the beautiful nature, and the Japanese culture – which is so very interesting to me." – responded the journalist.

"And what is one quality of the Japanese people that you praise above all others?" – asked Master Hakuin.

"Hmmm... Let me see..." – started the journalist. "Probably, that they are always very punctual and usually keep their promises!" – answered the journalist.

Mumon's comment:

In the world of chaos, Zen practitioners try to control their monkey-mind and tame their horse-will by being disciplined and keeping their promises.

Rock solid!

An Interpretation

I am sitting in my school right now and waiting for a student. The student is already 30 minutes late. I suppose that she won't show up today at all! The student is not Japanese. I have several non-Japanese students in my school in Japan. I won't mention their nationalities, because I don't want to create any negative stereotypes or sound racist in any way. I respect people of all creeds and nationalities. However, according to my experience thus far, the Japanese students are usually a lot more reliable than the students of other nationalities. Why is it so? I guess it's their upbringing: order and discipline are of the utmost importance in Japan. If a Japanese student is going to skip a class, he or she informs me about it prior to the class time, by an email, a text message, or a phone call. For the Japanese students a scheduled lesson comes first over most social engagements. The reason to cancel a class is usually serious and mostly due to some illness. It is rare for the Japanese students to cancel their classes. On the other hand, for some of my non-Japanese students it is easy to miss a class. The reasons for skipping a class include: a sudden visit by a friend, being tired, being invited to a party organized by friends, a picnic, a BBQ, and almost any other social engagement. Hence, I never know if in fact I will have a class that day or not...

For the Japanese people appointments are usually written in stone. They arrive at the place of the meeting a few minutes early and wait in their cars to enter the building where the meeting is held at the very precise time. Most Japanese are just like their public transportation – completely reliable and punctual to the minute. I must say that I treasure this reliability and punctuality as one of the best social qualities of the Japanese people.

Our world is a very uncertain place, our lives are very iffy, and our minds change easily. Hence, the ability to rely on someone's word makes this world safer and easier to live in.

Monkey-mind and *horse-will* mentioned by Mumon are Zen terms pertaining to the natural tendency of humans to change their mind, to be restless, and often torn up by desires. It is one the main points of Zen practice to calm the natural restlessness and to extinguish the desires which bring about frustration and dissatisfaction.

Ask yourself:

1. Do you usually keep your promises? Do you like it when other people keep their promises? How do you feel when others break their promises?

2. Are your countrymen usually reliable and punctual? Is the public transportation in your country reliable? Is your government reliable?

3. What social qualities do you prefer – being joyful and friendly towards everyone, but unreliable, or being socially reserved and timid, but reliable?

4. On one hand, it is good to be open-minded and flexible, and to easily adapt to the changing reality. On the other hand, it is good to remain steady in one's hopes, dreams, and plans. Think about the pros and the cons of being steadfast and of easily changing one's mind.

Nobody Is Perfect

"In order to seek enlightenment – Siddhartha Gautama Buddha abandoned his young wife and his child. Was that a moral action?" – asked Mondai.

"Well, Siddhartha was a prince, so his wife and child were never in any financial distress..." – responded Master Hakuin.

"But what about the wife's need for her husband and the child's need for the father?" – asked Mondai.

"I hate the sun!" – responded Master Hakuin.

"Why?" – asked Mondai.

"Because it has just murdered my snowman!" – said Master Hakuin.

.　　　.　　　.　　　.　　　.

Mumon's comment:

Trees are perhaps the most compassionate beings of all! They live off of minerals and sunshine, and normally they are very peaceful. But even trees can become killers of careless motorcyclists.

Watch out! An ant under your shoe sole!

Sun – the Assassin

An Interpretation

We live in an imperfect world... or anyway it seems so from our perspective. Perhaps from the perspective of God this world is completely just and perfect. Perhaps every hair on everyone's head is counted and accounted for. "Mene, Mene, Tekel, Upharsin." – we read in the Bible. "Everything is numbered, weighed and divided." (These words magically appeared on the wall of King Belshazzar's palace, meaning that the future of the king and his kingdom has been decided.)

Perhaps there is a divine justice, but it is hard to see it from the human perspective. It is hard to see the purpose of all the suffering that takes place on our planet. This is why Siddhartha Gautama Buddha set out on a quest for salvation and in the process of doing so, he hurt his immediate family.

When we want to drink tea or coffee – we boil water. It is impossible to boil water without killing a large number of microorganisms in it. It is impossible to drive a car without killing insects on the windshield and under the tires. We must try to do our best not to harm other beings, but as long as our forms are physical – we are bound to cause suffering in this world. The best we can do is to try to minimize it. "Thou shall avoid killing and harming other beings as much as thou can!" – should be our maxim in life. It means that we have to always compromise.

The Dalai Lama said: "When a mosquito comes to bite me – at first I move my arm away. If the mosquito returns – I try to wave it away with my hand. If it comes again – I flick it with my finger." Of course a flick of a finger may cause some damage or even kill the mosquito, but we have the right to protect ourselves... and to protect those who are in our care. Mosquitos kill more people in the world than all the wars combined.

Personally, I catch mosquitos in glasses when they show up in my house and after a while I release them outside. However, when I go for a dog walk I can't protect my dogs while being gentle to mosquitos. Mosquitos in Japan carry heartworms that kill dogs. So, sadly, I choose to kill mosquitos to protect my dogs. I know that I should vaccinate all my pets every summer against heartworms, but the cost is hard to bear...

We live in the world of compromises. When you save a spider – you condemn some flies the spider will kill in its lifetime. When you save a homeless, hungry kitten – you condemn some mice and maybe some birds the cat will catch in its lifetime. When you save a baby-bird – you condemn some insects and earthworms the bird will eat in its lifetime. How can we help all beings?

Ask yourself:

1. When you choose a romantic partner you have to reject other people. Can you do it without hurting them?

2. Some people think that choosing a handsome or a beautiful romantic partner is selfish and shallow, and that we should choose a partner who has a good character instead. But if you end up living with a partner you are not fully satisfied with, will you not hurt your partner by not giving him or her enough love?

3. God loves everyone, but if a human loves everyone – everyone is jealous! Is it okay to make people jealous? Aren't we hurting other people when we make them jealous?

4. How much of your free time and of your money should you dedicate to helping others and how much time and money should you spend on making yourself happy?

5. If experiencing pleasure gives you happiness and energy and therefore makes you more capable of helping others, should you indulge in pleasure? If so, to what degree?

6. If another man is romantically interested in the woman that you are also interested in, should you think of his feelings and try not to hurt him? Should you let him win the woman's heart or should you try to be a winner? Should you consider which relationship would be better for the woman or should you think only of what you want?

7. Should you choose the most unpleasant, difficult or dangerous tasks and duties, or should you selfishly protect yourself and delegate others to perform the needed, but very unpleasant or difficult tasks and duties? For example: should you always clean the toilet, or should you ask your wife to do it? If you see a burning building, should you be the one to run in and try to rescue others, or should you wait in safety for the "professional" rescuers?

The Mystic Pizza

"Master, how can meditation help us understand the world? How can looking into oneself help us understand what is outside of oneself?"– asked Mondai.

"Here, try this pizza!" – said Master Hakuin offering Mondai a piece of his dinner.

"Thanks!" – said Mondai and took a bite. "It's yummy!"

"What is it made of?" – asked Master Hakuin.

"I think... olives, mushrooms, green peppers, tomatoes, some spices, and, of course, the dough!" – answered Mondai.

"That's right!" – said Master Hakuin. "So you know what this piece is made of and how it tastes. Do you think that the rest of the pizza is made differently or has a different taste?"

"I guess it's all the same!" – said Mondai.

"And it is the same with meditation!" – said Master Hakuin.

.   .   .   .   .

Mumon's comment:

If you want to know something about the nature of God – study God's creation. If you want to discover the Universe – look deeply within yourself.

No meat, no cheese – pizza!

An Interpretation

Is there a good reason to think that the Universe is like a Big Pizza, and that studying a small piece of it, for example – oneself, can reveal useful information about the rest of the Universe? The mystics and many modern-day scientists think so.

Atoms inside our bodies are composed of subatomic particles spinning inside them. If the subatomic particles were the size of small pebbles – they would be spinning inside an area (an atom) which then would be the size of a football field. Hence, those tiny pebbles are surrounded by a lot of "empty space" and they cannot "fill it out", because they are so much smaller than the space in which they spin. Furthermore, the subatomic particles themselves are also composed of mostly "empty space". All in all, the subatomic physics inform us that matter is composed of pure energy!

What does it mean to us in the "human world"? It means that we – humans, all animals, plants, and even the inanimate matter (if matter is ever inanimate), such as minerals – are all made out of the same energy. The same God Energy created all there is! It would logically follow that studying one form of energy – a human being – can reveal a great deal about other forms of energy – the rest of the world. Don't you agree?

We can imagine human body as the sky above us. If we enlarged it a great deal, there would be vast space between the stars and the planets – the spinning subatomic particles. We can think of a human body as the Universe, and we can think of the Universe as a living creature! Plato and other Ancient Greek philosophers thought that the universe might be a living being, perhaps shaped like a sphere... The space is curved – confirm the scientist. Perhaps we live inside a Giant Apple? Perhaps the wormholes are indeed made by worms?☺

Ask yourself:

1. Do you ever think of your body as a universe of atoms and subatomic particles which may be inhabited by extremely small creatures? In fact, your body is a world for an enormous number of microorganisms. Do you have any sense of responsibility towards them?☺

2. If the Earth is a living organism, what do you think the Earth "thinks" of humans? Are humans welcome and useful organisms to the Earth, or are we parasites to this planet?

3. Human beings cut down the forests, pollute the waters and the air, and "suck out" the blood of the Earth (oil). Is there any wonder that the Earth wants to get rid of us by flooding, earthquakes, droughts, and other natural disasters? When hostile microorganisms attack your body, how does your body defend itself?

4. Have you ever discovered anything about other people by observing yourself? If so, what have you discovered in this way?

5. To what extent are non-human animals similar to human beings? Can animals feel and think? Should animals have the same right not to be harmed as humans do?

Zen Miracles

"Master Hakuin, can a Zen practitioner acquire some supernatural powers and perform miracles?" – asked Mondai.

"When a baby bird wants to learn how to fly – it sits in the nest for a few weeks and practices Zazen. One day, when it is fully covered in feathers – it jumps out of the nest and it can fly!" – said Master Hakuin.

"When a child wants to learn how to walk – it must first sit in a bed or a stroller for a few months and practice Zazen. Eventually the child acquires the power to walk on two legs!" – continued Master Hakuin.

"But these are normal abilities, not supernatural powers!" – said Mondai.

Master Hakuin stretched out his arm in the air. Instantly a dragonfly came by and landed on Master Hakuin's hand.

"Everything is normal when you know how to do it!" – said Master Hakuin.

.   .   .   .   .

Mumon's Comment:

It is the supernatural power of the Buddha, the Bodhisattvas, and of all the enlightened beings to be aware of the fact that life is a miracle indeed!

To befriend a dragonfly is a miracle!

An Interpretation

What is a miracle? It is an extraordinary act of God. Isn't all life an extraordinary act of God?

In the beginning there was the Energy. There was the Desire to Exist. This Desire came together in a powerful Ball of Energy and exploded as Big Bang – the beginning of the entire Universe. As time passed by (but what is time?) the Universe grew and out of the soup of the cosmic dust our planet emerged. Probably many planets like ours emerged out of the soup of the cosmic dust... On the numerous planets like ours this cosmic dust started to form creatures. Living creatures started to crawl, walk, fly and swim in the waters of the planets like ours. As time passed by (but what is time?) the creatures evolved and some of them became rather sophisticated. Some of them started to make cars and planes, and TVs. They invented numbers and letters. They started to calculate all sorts of things and to write books. The cosmic dust that does math, writes books, and flies airplanes – is quite miraculous indeed!...

The cosmic dust in the form of the creatures feels happy to be alive. But it also often feels lonely, frightened and confused. Every time one particle of the cosmic dust consoles another particle – it is a miracle. Any act of compassion is a miracle!...

Do we need to defy the Laws of the Miraculous Universe to believe in miracles? Do we need to see the fish drive cars and the humans walk on water to believe that we are the miraculous creation of the Divine Energy?

Ask yourself:

1. Since the ancient times people have unsuccessfully tried to make a machine that wouldn't require any external source of energy. Such a machine is called *perpetuum mobile* or a *perpetual motion machine*. Isn't the Universe in its entirety such a machine? If the Universe is nothing but the Energy, then is life real? Buddhist say that life is and isn't at the same time. How do you understand this statement?

2. Is a rainbow real? What is a rainbow? Is love real? What is love?

3. You are now on Earth (unless you are an astronaut reading this book in a spaceship!☺ Or unless a few thousand years have passed since this book was written, and humans have colonized some other planets. In which case – congratulations!☺) and this planet is inside the Milky Way galaxy, and the Milky Way galaxy is inside the Universe. But where is the Universe? Where are you now? Who or what are you now? When is now? (As already mentioned in this book – NOW HERE is NOWHERE!)

4. When you board an airplane and the airplane doesn't fall down and kill you – it is so, because God performs a miracle and protects you, just like He (She or It) protected Daniel in the lion's den. Every day of your life you are protected by God.

Of course one day – you will die, because this is God's plan too... Do you feel protected every day of your life? Isn't God's protection of your life a miracle?

5. Do you ever think of the flowers around you as miracles? Do you ever look at ants or fruit flies and think of them as miracles? When you feel very lonely and an ant shows up on the floor in front of you, or a butterfly sits on your knee – do you know that God has just sent a messenger to cheer you up and say: "Don't worry – you are NEVER alone!"? When you feel very lonely and you call your friend, and he or she agrees to meet you, and have a cake and coffee with you – do you ever think of this event as a miracle?... If you don't– then think again!☺

6. Our children (human or animal) are here to experience life. They are also here to cheer us up and to nurture our compassion and love. Sometimes it is hard to appreciate children as God's miracles, because they require much care and attention. Sometimes we get tired of their cries, and we feel frustrated because of their complaints, but overall we should perceive them as miracles. Especially when we get old – children cheer us up and give us new energy and new will to live. Do you think so?

7. It is a known fact that people who have pets live longer than people who have no companions. Why do you think it is so?

In Kyoto's Garden

One day, Master Hakuin and his students went to Kyoto, and decided to sit in Zazen in one of the Japanese traditional gardens. During the meditation, Josei suddenly broke her composure and said:

"Master Hakuin, I hear the sound of heavenly music! Is it coming from my deep meditational state?"

"No!" – responded Master Hakuin. "It's coming from those speakers over there, hooked up to the Cultural Center behind the garden."

Mumon's comment:

Sometimes the answer is as easy as a bird in the tree.

... Is a bird in the tree – easy?

An Interpretation

Josei is a very sensitive person. Despite Master Hakuin's simple explanation, it is possible that Josei heard the music of her soul, or perhaps even the music of the heavenly spheres. Actually, the way we perceive music is of course very personal and individual. That is why for some people the instrumental music of Yanni, Vollenweider, or Vangelis sounds heavenly, and for others it is simply boring. Personally, I can't imagine how it is possible not to be deeply moved and uplifted by the music of the three, abovementioned musicians, but to my surprise they are virtually unknown in Japan. And whenever I play some of their music to my students it falls on deaf ears!... Perhaps it is a question of upbringing. But then again, who am I to criticize my students when I fall asleep at the concerts of Chopin and even Mozart... (Though I do love the movie by Milos Forman titled *Amadeus!*) Perhaps it is a question of upbringing and of timing!...

Ask yourself:

1. What state of mind do classical concerts or opera performances require? What state of mind do rock or pop concerts require? Can a spiritually developed person dislike classical music? Personally, I am not very fond of some of the "sleepy" classical composers, but I enjoy some livelier pieces (of Rachmaninoff, Ravel, Beethoven, etc.) and especially I like New Age music of Yanni, Vollenweider, Vangelis, Kitaro, etc. What is your favorite kind of music and why do you like it?

2. It is said that plants grow better when they are exposed to classical music. Do you think so? Have you ever played music to the plants in your care?

3. Does music have an impact on human health? Can unsettling or distressing music cause a disease? Can harmonious music speed up someone's recovery?

4. What do you think of the "music" that claims to worship the devil? What do you think of the gangster rap "music" which talks about killing people, drugs, prostitution, etc.? Does music influence the imagination of our children? To some degree music is censored and controlled by the laws of the countries in which it is made – so we usually don't see any real violence in music videos. But is some radical, modern music harmless enough? Rapping about violent crimes against women, such as beating, raping, and killing – has a deeply desensitizing effect on the society. Do the songs of many popular rappers instill chauvinism in their fans?

5. Have you heard of Ani Choying Drolma? She is a singing Buddhist nun. Her songs are very popular in Nepal. Do you know of any other popular spiritual musicians?

6. Nature has its own music. Do you like the sound of ocean waves? Do you enjoying listening to the whispers of mountain streams? Do you like the crackling sound of camp fire? What sounds of nature do you like best and why? Are there any sounds of nature that you dislike? Are you afraid of rumbling thunders?

7. Which animal sounds make you feel most comfortable and which ones make you feel most distressed and why? (For example: purring of a cat, howling of a wolf, hooting of an owl, hissing of a snake, crowing of a rooster, screeching of a hawk, etc.)

Japanese gardens are truly inspirational.

Master Henjin's Dragon Fire

After many years of meditation Master Henjin developed the ability to breathe fire out of his mouth.

"Master Hakuin, do you think that I can ever achieve this level of spiritual development?" – asked Mondai.

"Breathing fire out of one's mouth is easy. Extinguishing it – is one of the true purposes of practicing Zen!" – answered Master Hakuin.

Mumon's comment:

Angry fire can burn down half a forest. But when the fire is raging – how can you save the animals and the trees?

An Interpretation

This story is reminiscent of the famous Buddhist story about the yogi who could walk on water. When Buddha came to the bank of a certain river, he met there a yogi who was able to walk on water. The yogi proudly displayed his supernatural ability to Buddha.

"How long has it taken you to learn this skill?" – asked Buddha.

"About 30 years." – answered the yogi.

"What a waste of time! You could have paid a ferryman just 10 rupees to take you across the river!" – responded Buddha.

"Henjin" in Japanese means a "strange person". It is strange and unnecessary to try to develop supernatural powers when one hasn't yet fully mastered the natural skills and abilities. "Breathing out fire" is easy, because expressing anger is easy. We all shout and "breathe out fire" when we get angry. Master Hakuin says that one of the main objects of practicing Zen is to learn how to control one's anger. A person who can control one's anger and perhaps even calm down others – is spiritually far more advanced than a man who can "imitate dragons". Mumon adds that anger can bring about a lot of harm to sentient beings. Uncontrolled anger is one of the causes of evil.

Ask yourself:

1. Do you often get angry? If so, why?

2. Have you heard of anger management classes? Do you know any of the techniques suggested in such classes? (Visualizing a relaxing place, repeating a calming phrase, etc.) Do you try to control your anger? If so, how?

3. Sometimes anger can bring about a positive outcome. For example in the New Testament, Jesus got angry at the animal sellers conducting their business in the synagogue, and he expressed his anger by shouting and chasing them out. Money

making and killing animals as a sacrifice has nothing to do with worshipping God! Do you ever get angry for a righteous cause? How should we express anger in a constructive manner?

4. In The Old Testament, God's wrath brings about the destructive flood. In the New Testament, God is loving, patient, understanding, and forgiving. What is a better life motto — "an eye for an eye" or "forgiveness"?

5. Many insects live for a very short time. Adult dragonflies live for about four months. Houseflies live for about four weeks. Adult mayflies live only one day! All these insects have no time to get angry!☺ Is human life really that much longer? Isn't life too short to get angry? When we are young – we think that life is long, but when we are old – we know better. Does life seem long or short to you?

6. It is evident that on average people who get easily angry have shorter lifespans than those who are easygoing. Why do you think it is so?

7. Many Zen masters of the past had long lives. Can Zazen contribute to longevity? If so, why?

Omiyage

When Master Hakuin returned from his week-long travel around Japan he entered the monastery at the time of the evening meditation. Although all the masters and the disciples were deeply engaged in practicing Zazen, the monastery became instantly filled with wild clamor. Master Hakuin's dogs were greeting him barking, howling, and whimpering; his cats were meowing and purring; his chickens were crowing and cackling; and his rabbits were happily running in circles and occasionally stomping the floor with their hind legs. All animals were charged with excitement and filled with delight. Master Hakuin looked at his quiet and motionless disciples and colleagues and at his noisy and swarming animals – and said:

"A single outcry of love is better than a hundred thousand years of sitting meditation!"

He fed his animals heartily and opened a bottle of sake for himself.

.   .   .   .   .

Mumon's comment:

Like Ikkyu, Master Hakuin is a passionate man. Whenever he returns from a voyage – he always brings snacks for his animals, but hardly ever any omiyage (souvenirs) for his colleagues and disciples. No wonder they don't greet him!

Master Hakuin's venerable colleagues

An Interpretation

Omiyage is a souvenir from a trip. Usually it is something small and inexpensive. It may be a paper fan, a keychain, or a fridge magnet, but most often it is some kind of food or drink. Japanese sweets make for a great omiyage!

In Japan, omiyage is so customary that one may feel offended not to get at least a candy or a rice cracker from a friend who had been away on a trip. However, Zen masters and Zen disciples shouldn't indulge in earthly pleasures. A staple diet at a Zen monastery usually consists of a bowl of rice and some tea. Perhaps then Master Hakuin was not wrong to return home without any presents for his colleagues?

And why does Mumon compare Master Hakuin to Ikkyu? Master Ikkyu was famous for having strong opinions and being fond of sake!

Should Zen Masters ever indulge in drinking sake?

Ask yourself:

1. When we see the multitude of beliefs in the world – we can choose those beliefs that seem the most admirable or profitable. Traveling helps discover the beliefs in the world. Do you like to travel? If so, what have you discovered from your recent travels?

2. Traveling can be physical or mental. Reading books, surfing the internet, watching movies, and talking to other people – are all forms of mental travelling. What have you discovered lately from your mental travels?

3. "Every person is a world to be discovered." – do you agree with this saying?

4. The most satisfying conversations are those that reveal the paths of human mind – the ways of thinking and the values we uphold. Do you enjoy talking with other people? If so, why? Are you truly interested in the minds of other people, or are you mostly interested in showing off your own mind? Or you predominantly a talker or also a listener?

Who Is Ikkyu? Who Is Mumon?

Having read the previous story Mondai asked:

"Who is or was Ikkyu?"

Mumon answered:

"Ikkyu was a famous rebel monk who lived in the 15th century and received his education in several Zen temples in Kyoto. When he became an adult he gave up the monastic lifestyle. He spent much time in brothels with lovers and sake, and he wrote many poems."

"I see! Thanks for that!" – said Mondai. "By the way, who are you?"

"I am not sure who Mumon is" – replied Mumon – "but there seems to be Mumon as a commentator in many Zen books..."

"I see!" – said Mondai with a very silly smile on his face.

Mumon smiled too, and a strange silence filled the room... and the book!

SILENCE

An Interpretation

The painting of Ikkyu (left) and the sculpture of Ikkyu (right) can be seen in Ikkyuji – a complex of Zen temples located in Kyotanabe city and built by Ikkyu. The complex was originally built as a Zen monastery. Some of the beautiful gardens surrounding the pavilions were designed by Murata Juko – the founder of the wabi style tea ceremony. Ikkyu-ji is famous for fermented natto beans – for which the recipe is supposed to have been handed down by master Ikkyu himself.

Zen master Ikkyu was born in 1394 and died in 1481. He was a very colorful figure, who attracted attention of many Japanese artists of his time. He was an illegitimate child of the emperor and grew up in Zen monasteries. What is the most shocking and perhaps also very appealing to many of his followers is that Ikkyu was a rebel and acted in a very unorthodox manner. He was known to often drink wine and spend time with prostitutes in brothels. Many modern Zen practitioners in the West think of Ikkyu as one of the most influential figures in the history of the Japanese Zen Buddhism.

For the Japanese, Ikkyu is famous as a hero of stories for children. The story of Ikkyu and a tiger is particularly famous:

When Ikkyu was a child, he was a very clever boy. The lord of the nearby lands heard of Ikkyu's wit and decided to test him. He invited Ikkyu to his house and showed him a folding screen with a picture of a tiger on it. "I am very tired and scared of this tiger's growling at night. Can you help me catch him?" – the lord asked Ikkyu. "Give me a rope." – Ikkyu said. When he got the rope, Ikkyu made a lasso and said: "I am now ready to catch the tiger, just please chase him out of the screen!" The lord liked Ikkyu's witty response and gave him many presents in reward.

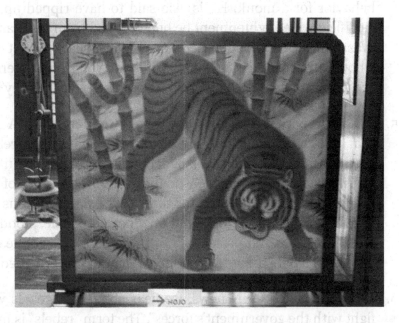

A screen with a tiger in a bamboo forest.

Ask yourself:

1. Do you like rebel-type characters? If so, why? If not, why not?

2. Do you remember James Dean's movie – *Rebel without a Cause*? Why do you think it is so famous?

3. In the *Oxford Dictionary of English* there is a separate entry for "a rebel without a cause". This expression is defined as "a person who is dissatisfied with the society, but does not have a specific aim to fight for". Actually, in the movie – *Rebel without a Cause*, the main characters (Jim Stark, Judy, and Plato) are mostly dissatisfied with their parents. In any case, being dissatisfied with life in general can be remedied by Zen, or so Master Hakuin would have us believe. What are some of the things you are dissatisfied with?

4. Ikkyu didn't care much about what other people thought about him. Drinking and womanizing was (and is) not an acceptable behavior for a monk. He is also said to have ripped up the certificate of enlightenment he had received from his master. Was James Dean popular because of his laid back, "don't give a hoot" attitude? Are you laid back, or are you rather intense? Which character type is more interesting to you and why?

5. In Japan there is a saying: "Deru kugi wa utareru" – "A nail that sticks out gets hammered down." Sometimes rebel-type characters make other people angry. Can you think of examples of famous people who didn't follow the rules of the society and got persecuted for that? (For example: Jesus ate and socialized with simple and uneducated people, stood up for a prostitute and protected her from being stoned, healed people on a Sabbath, etc., and for all that he was crucified.)

6. When we watch CNN news, we hear about "the rebels who fight with the government's forces". The term "rebels" is most often used to denote an armed opposition to the government. We rarely think of Copernicus as a rebel, but in fact he was one. Any scientist or a thinker who comes up with an idea that is new and different from the accepted ones – is a rebel. Martin Luther King was a rebel. Feminists are rebels. Vegetarians are rebels. Are you a rebel too?

7. We can think of Gautama Siddhartha Buddha as a rebel too. Buddha rejected many religious and cultural beliefs and traditions of his time. For example, we are told that he didn't accept the elevation of the high priests over other people. He didn't accept the division of the society into casts. He allowed women into the sanga (the community of monks and nuns), etc. According to Buddhism – we are all equal. This attitude is very noble, but it is hard to find in modern work environment – where the bosses are often superior to their employees. Do you ever elevate yourself over other people? For example, when you go to a convenience store – do you treat the clerks as your equals, or do you treat them as your servants? Do you treat your kids or your spouse as your equals?

Buddhism: "We are all equal!"

Ofuro - Eureka!

One day Mondai said:

"Master Hakuin, I spend an hour in ofuro (Japanese bath) every day, but I can't relax deeply or come up with any profound thoughts while in the bath, because I sweat too much and simply feel uncomfortable. Is ofuro useful to a Zen practitioner?"

"Well, in ancient Greece Archimedes experienced satori (eureka) while he was in a bath!... Perhaps your water temperature is too high?" – responded Master Hakuin.

The following day Mondai came to Master Hakuin and said:

"Master Hakuin, today I lowered the water temperature. It was almost cold, yet I still had no profound thoughts. Is there anything else I should change in the bath?"

"Perhaps you should change the bather!" – responded Master Hakuin.

.   .   .   .   .

Mumon's comment:

You can bring a camel to water, but you can't make it come up with the law of buoyancy!

However, after many years of experimenting with ofuro Mondai formulated his own law:

"The apparent loss in weight of a body immersed in water is equal to the weight of the water displaced by this body... plus about one kilogram of sweat, if you stay in the bath for an hour and if the water is very hot."

A square-shaped, deep bathtub to sit in.

An Interpretation

Of course Mondai was right! If you stay for a while in a bath of hot water – you sweat like crazy, and after an hour you lose at least a litter of sweat. Furthermore, as a result of sweating, your skin unclogs and you eliminate some of the waste stored in your body – heavy metals, harmful chemicals and fat. As a result – you become healthier and slimmer!

The health benefits of ohuro are well-known in Japan, and especially the Japanese ladies use baths as means of controlling weight and keeping their skin smooth and silky. In general, the Japanese people are a slim, although with the introduction of the Western fast food chains, such as McDonalds and Kentucky Fried Chicken – more and more Japanese become obese.

These days I weight around eighty kilograms, which is quite appropriate for someone my height (187cm), but when I just came to Japan I weighed twenty kilograms more. In Canada, being quite tall and weighing one hundred kilograms was not so bad in comparison with other people. Many adult Canadians and Americans are as round as donuts! However, in Japan I was instantly labelled: "the fat teacher".

In North America, being fat is thought of as either quite normal or as an unfortunate ailment that can't be helped. We are told that fat people should not be discriminated against, and we shouldn't even call them "fat", because it sounds demeaning or offensive. Instead, in a politically correct language, fat people are called "big" or "full-figured". Who is to benefit from the social belief that being fat is normal or necessary? Of course, the food makers – the big companies that turn us into sugar and AAAs – artificial additives addicts! While they make billions of dollars, we (the consumers) believe that we ought to buy and consume their unhealthy products!

In Japan, being fat is looked down at and thought of as being untidy, gluttonous, and lacking discipline. Japanese people are expected to be slim (except for the sumo fighters, who are supposed to be as fat as they can get).

The size of the traditional Japanese meals and drinks is much smaller than the size of the Western servings, which naturally helps keep the weight down. When I first bought a canned drink in Japan – it seemed to me like a thimble. I had to have at least three of them to feel satisfied. Nowadays, Big Gulp at McDonalds and Latte Grande at Starbucks begin to change the size preferences of the young Japanese. If the trend continues – even ohuro may not be of much help...

Ask yourself:

1. Is being overweight as a sign of gluttony, a personal preference, or a disease?

2. Should obesity be protected and spoken of in euphemistic terms, or should it be discouraged by the use of derogatory terms?

3. Have you seen the movie titled *Shallow Hal*? In this movie a man who likes to date good looking, slim women, is magically transformed to perceive a hugely overweight woman as slim and sexy. Is it shallow to think of overweight people as less attractive than slim people?

Ikebana

"Pretty flowers, aren't they?" – said Pretty Rose pointing at the ikebana arrangement she has just made.

"Yes, almost as pretty as you are!" – responded Master Hakuin with a smile.

"Do you want these flowers in your bedroom?" – asked Pretty Rose.

"I don't like crowds! One Pretty Rose is enough!" – answered Master Hakuin.

.   .   .   .   .

Mumon's comment:

Everyone likes pretty flowers, but flowers look best where they can thrive.

Leave the flowers where they grow, and they shall be thankful to you for the rest of their lives!

Ikebana

An Interpretation

Esthetically, ikebana can be very pleasing, but when I think of flowers detached from their roots, stuck on nails, and just "gasping for air" for the last time – I feel that painting or photography are far more gratifying forms of art.

When I lived in Norway, I met there an ascetic, named Bjorn (which means "bear" in Norwegian). Bjorn had lived in the same spot (near the University of Oslo), under the open sky, for some fifteen years. To many people he was just a crazy, homeless man, who lived in the park, but to me and to some of his friends and followers he was a mystic with an interesting insight on life. One day, Bjorn talked to me about the flowers that grew all around him. "Be careful not to step on any of them!" – he said. "These flowers are my friends and I don't want them to be harmed in any way!" Bjorn's love for all living creatures, including plants, was very reminiscent of the compassion of Saint Francis of Assisi! Knowingly or unknowingly, Bjorn had practiced Zen, day in and day out, 24 hours a day, for those fifteen years he had lived in the park.

I think that cutting down an evergreen tree in order to place it in one's room, decorate it with Christmas ornaments, and watch it dry and die in the span of a couple of months – is even worse than cutting flowers. After all, if left alone, trees can easily outlive human beings. Is killing a tree a good way to celebrate the birth of Jesus Christ?

And why do we express our love by giving cut and dying roses (or other flowers) to those we care for? Why not give them seashells or pretty stones, or cones – instead? The Rose in *The Little Prince* would not approve of such behavior. Nor does Master Hakuin!

Ask yourself:

1. Do you like to see flowers growing in nature? If so, why?

2. Have you ever given or received cut flowers? If so, what did it make you feel like? Would you hesitate to throw freshly cut flowers into fire? Would you hesitate to cut down a tree? If so, why?

3. Is it possible that plants have feelings? What evidence have you come across in support of plants' sentience (their ability to feel pain and pleasure)?

4. Have you read the book by Christopher Bird and Peter Tompkins, titled *The Secret Life of Plants*? In this book, the authors talk about the CIA and the KGB researches into plants' consciousness. The authors of the book provide a lot of evidence in support of plants' sentience, and show that plants may even have more developed cognitive skills – such memory and recognition of other beings. How would you change your attitude towards plants, if you knew (with certainty) that they can think and feel?

5. Of course, we presently know (with absolute certainty) that animals can feel and think, and yet, we slaughter them and eat them. If you had to slaughter a pig or to cut up a carrot – what would you rather do, and why?

Get-a Balance!

"Master Hakuin, do you practice judo?" – asked Mondai.

"No, I don't. Why do you ask?" – responded Master Hakuin.

"Because one of your geta sandals (traditional Japanese sandals) seems to have only one tooth (one of the two wooden blocks attached to the sandal underneath the sole). It must be for practicing your balance, right?" – said Mondai.

"That's right! It's for practicing my **mental** balance!" – replied Master Hakuin.

.   .   .   .   .

Mumon's comment:

How can one-toothed geta help in balancing the mind? If you have no glue or no time to mend an old shoe – must you get stressed out about it? Sometimes simply not worrying – helps your mental balance! Geta Balance!

Geta sandals

An Interpretation

Traditionally Japanese judo fighters practice their balance walking in one-toothed geta sandals.

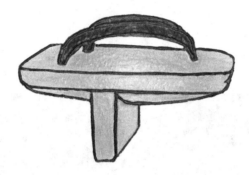

It's pretty similar to walking in skates.

When I was a teenager I practiced judo for a while. My teacher advised me to practice balance by free standing (without any hand support) while riding buses, trains, and other public transportation vehicles (such as trams or trolleys).

Master Hakuin doesn't practice judo and his single-toothed geta sandal was created accidentally, simply because one tooth fell off. Why doesn't Master Hakuin repair his sandal or buy new ones? Perhaps he wants to challenge himself for a while, or as he told his student – it is a form of "letting go" and remaining in a relaxed state of mind even while facing adversities or discomfort.

I remember having asked Bjorn (the ascetic who lived under the open sky in Oslo, Norway) why he didn't move to a warmer country to practice his asceticism. "Wouldn't it be easier to live in a warmer climate, for example on Mt. Athos in Greece?" – I asked. "I don't need to seek a warmer climate, because warm weather comes to me every summer!" – answered Bjorn.

It is not easy to accept and tolerate the hardships of life. It is the kind of learning we all could benefit from!

Ask yourself:

1. Have you ever accepted some discomforts in life in order to simply challenge yourself? Have you ever tried to live like an ascetic? Are you sensitive to harsh weather, lack of food, hard physical work, etc.? Are you a tough person?

2. When I was a teenager I tried to overcome pain. At times I tested my resistance to pain. For example, I kept my hand next to a very hot radiator until I got a burnt mark. Have you ever tried to tolerate pain (for example, by letting a dentist drill in your tooth without anesthetics)? What could be the purpose of such a challenge?

3. Here is a challenge: Whenever you want to cry, look up in the sky (you can look through the ceiling) and say: "Dear God, thank you for testing my inner strength! Look how powerful I am! I feel like crying, but I am going to smile!" And smile! What do you think about this challenge? Is it a good way to overcome depression?

4. What do you do when you feel mentally unbalanced – when you feel anxious, nervous, worried, or depressed?

Shinkansen

One day, Master Hakuin and his disciple Hayaku were traveling by shinkansen – the bullet train – from Kyoto to Tokyo.

The trip was very fast and lasted only a little over two hours. If one goes by car – the same trip takes five to six hours.

When they arrived in Tokyo, Hayaku said: "I wish the trip to enlightenment was like taking a shinkansen train – smooth, quiet, comfortable, and very fast!"

"I am glad the trip to enlightenment is long and arduous – like taking a bicycle or walking!" – said Master Hakuin.

"But, master!" – exclaimed Hayaku – "Why do you prefer the world to evolve slowly?"

"Because I like the smell of the autumn grasses and the sound of the crying cranes!" – answered Master Hakuin.

Mumon's comment: If we were born as adults, we would never make origami, fly kites, and play with spinning tops or Gameboys.

An Interpretation

If we were born as adults in the Western countries – we would never play hopscotch, build sandcastles, eat lollipops, seek treasures, and read books about pirates! Childhood has its beauty in many cultures...

Mono no aware is the Japanese term for *enjoying life deeply* or *savoring life's beauty.*

The bullet train is fast and smooth, but it doesn't give us a chance to admire the flowers when we pass by, or to listen to the birds when we ride through the forests. When Kilgore Trout rode a shinkansen (or maybe it was Master Hakuin when he was young), he wrote the following poem☺ :

A Bullet Train

I'm riding on the bullet train
300 clicks and hour
I feel no pleasure and no pain
Only my feet smell sour.

This train for Tokyo must be bound
Much smoother than a bus
There almost isn't any sound...
Except for passing gas!

Mono no aware – savoring life's beauty

Ask yourself:

1. Do you like funny poems? Personally, I think that the above poem is a bit unsophisticated, or even somewhat crass, but since it is humorous – the author (Kilgore Trout or young Master Hakuin) can be forgiven! Remember – to have a funny bone is quite important for any "serious" Zen practitioner!☺

2. What life's beauty have you admired most recently? If you can't remember – please, LOOK AROUND YOU!

3. The painting below portrays elements of outstanding beauty of Japan – awesome nature – mountains and seas, beautiful women, and the Japanese technology – represented by a train. When you visit Japan – admire them all! Furthermore, mountains hold special significance in Shintoism (the

Japanese traditional religious beliefs) and mountain worship was widespread in feudal Japan.

What are the most beautiful features of your country?

The Beauty of Japan

Kagami (Mirror)

"Master Hakuin, do you know why in Shintoism (Japanese traditional religion) a mirror often symbolizes a deity?" – asked Mondai.

"As you are to others – so God is to you. Hence, God is your mirror image." – answered Master Hakuin.

.   .   .   .   .

Mumon's comment:

There are many Gods in Japan, but only one God in the World. How is it possible?

An ignorant child grows up to be a wise adult. Is the selfish child the same person as the altruistic grownup, or are they two different people? Are you one or many?

K
A
G
A
M
I

An Interpretation

In Christianity, we say that God created human beings in His image. Of course not only humans resemble God (or are God's children), but also "all living creatures are created in the image of God", or, as we would say it in Buddhism: "all living creatures have the Buddha-nature".

All beings participate in the process of the spiritual evolution – growing from the Seed of the Universe into the Tree of the Universe, and finally into the Sweet Fruit.

In Christianity, we are told to see God as The Holy Trinity – the Father, The Son, and the Holy Spirit. God the Father, or God the Creator, is the Power of Life. God the Son, or Loving Kindness, is the Fruit, or the Child of the Spiritual Evolution. Finally, God the Spirit, or God the Ruler, is the Law of Life.

Even though all beings possess the Buddha-nature – very few of them come to realize it and live in accordance with this realization. There are very few Bodhisattvas in the world. This is why the Buddha-nature is also like a mirror. The more we act in accordance with our Buddha-nature – the more we see it all around us. Perhaps we could put it like this: The more we are there for Buddha – the more Buddha is there for us!

Ask yourself:

1. What does it mean to you to be in God's image?

2. What qualities of character did Gautama Buddha possess? What was the Buddha like? What should a Bodhisattva be like? Do you try to be like the Buddha or the Bodhisattvas? If so, how?

3. One of the qualities of God is benevolence. Are you benevolent to others? Do you often act out of compassion? (For example,

when you see a hungry animal or a homeless person – do you stop and try to help them?)

4. Another important quality of God is creativity. God the Creator makes the whole world. Are you creative? If so, how?

5. A: How is it going?

B: Same old same old, and you?

A: All different and all new!

Are you an A–type or a B–type person?

6. How can you interpret the picture titled *Kagami* (*Mirror*)? Why is the face in the mirror both smiling and crying? Why is the mirror broken into many pieces?

7. Some philosophers and many Zen practitioners believe that the microcosm is the mirror image of the macrocosm. Is the Universe a mirror image of a human being? What other mirror images can you think of?

8. "What goes around comes around!" "You reap what you sow!" Do these two sayings express the principle of a mirror image (or reciprocity)? If so, how?

A Discovery

"After forty years of searching through the skies I have finally discovered a new star!" – shouted a scientist.

"Every day when I wake up and open my eyes I discover a whole new universe!" – whispered Master Hakuin.

Mumon's comment:

No two beings are alike. No two beings think, feel, and experience in exactly the same way.

Nothing stays unchanged. Nobody experiences exactly the same thing twice.

Hence, all experiences are always unique. They are all – discoveries!

Appreciate them!

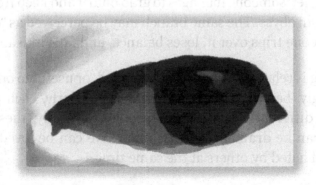

Every point of view is a new discovery

An Interpretation

Descartes and other rationalists don't trust our sensory perception. Our sight, hearing, the sense of touch, and our smell – may deceive us. The world around us may be different than what we perceive. Everything may be a mirage. We may be dreaming or hallucinating, or as Descartes put it: "we may be deceived by an evil daemon"...

In fact, every object appears differently from a different perspective and at a different moment in time. In the daytime, a tree looks serene and friendly, but at night, the same tree seems dangerous and scary.

Furthermore, each object appears differently to every person. My hands are used to heat, so a cup of soup seems lukewarm to me. A child's hands are more sensitive, so the same cup of soup seems hot in the hands of the child.

Our perception may differ depending on our mood. When we are happy, the day seems bright. When we're sad, it seems gloomy. Time passes by with different speed, depending on the circumstances we are in. When we are at the dentist, each minute seems like an hour. When we are with a loved one, the time flashes by like a lightning.

Depending on the circumstances the same object may be seen as a curse or a blessing. A branch of a tree may be seen as a "divine miracle", when someone manages to grab onto it and keep from falling down into an abyss. The same branch may be perceived as "demonic" when someone trips over it, loses balance, and falls into an abyss.

Everything is relative – what is nice, or good, or useful to one person, may be ugly, bad, or useless to another. Similarly, each person is perceived differently by different people. Naturally, these mental portraits can be dramatically dissimilar. We can be loved by some people and hated by others at the same time.

Every person is different at a different moment in time. Merciful and cruel, brave and cowardly, selfless and egoistic, wise and stupid – we all may be one and the other, at different times, depending on circumstances...

Rationalists believe that only reason can be relied upon. But reason too can be deceived and deceiving. Whatever we think – may be not the case. Every concept, every idea can be misconstrued. What certainty do we have that our understanding of an idea is correct?

Everything we can think of is linked to our previous experiences. Thus, when we think of any object, we relate it to our past. While a person living in a remote village in Asia, who hasn't heard of fascism, connects swastika only with Buddhism, a survivor of a Nazi concentration camp can never equate swastika with the symbol of the sun.

Every concept is understood differently by each person. Being patriotic, being pious, being moral, being a successful human being, being a good parent, being a good friend – all of these ideas mean totally different things to every one of us.

Every person perceives and imagines the world differently. In fact, we can say that every person lives in a different mental world. Every sentient being (humans and animals alike) constantly changes his or her mental world. Our mental worlds are constantly being remodeled and developed. We live in the multitude of worlds which keep changing like kaleidoscopes. Living, breathing, growing, being born and dying – forever changing the patterns of energy that surround us and create us.

Descartes thought that he could rely on his reason. "I think therefore I am!" – he exclaimed triumphantly. But is there an "I", which stands still – an "I", which can be pointed to? Every passing minute "I" change my understanding of the world around me. Every passing moment my awareness changes and becomes a different "I"...

"Panta rhei!"– said Heraclitus – "the world flows like a river"... But who can walk on water? We'd better be very careful about passing judgment, and about acting like we know it all!

Ask yourself:

1. What have you discovered lately?

2. Are you the same person now as you were in kindergarten? What has changed about you since the time of kindergarten?

3. What are your feelings now? Can you describe your feelings precisely? If you write how you feel in your diary today and look at this entry a year from now – will you be able to understand your feelings well, to the point of being able to recall or reconstruct them? Can we ever convey our feelings to other people?

4. What did you feel or think yesterday at 5 p.m.? Can you remember it? What did you feel or think exactly one hour ago? Is there a way to "freeze" our feelings or our thoughts? If all mental states constantly keep changing and we can't remember what they were even in the most recent past, and if we don't know what they will be in the near future, then what do we know about our mental states? Can we understand our own mental states? If not, then how can we know that there is a continuous self?

5. Would it be more valuable to you to discover something real about yourself, or to discover the existence of a distant star? (Of course if you are an astronomer – I am sure you will say that the latter is a lot more valuable to you...)

6. What is the most important discovery you have ever made? Here is mine:

A Philosophical Question

When a Western philosopher met Master Hakuin, he said:

"In Western philosophy, there is one fundamental question that needs to be answered. The question is: *What is the meaning of life?*

So, what is the fundamental Zen question?"

Master Hakuin replied:

"I had been married three times, yet I am still puzzled by the same fundamental question: *What is the meaning of wife?*"

.   .   .   .   .

Mumon's comment:

Master Hakuin is not Socrates and Pretty Rose is not Xantippe. Though they both could be!

And what is the fundamental question for a dyslectic theologian? *How to prove the existence of Dog!*

An Interpretation

Master Hakuin tells the Western philosopher that the fundamental Zen problem is the meaning of wife. I hope that the Western philosopher has a sense of humor. If not, he might misunderstand Master Hakuin's answer. Why did Mumon mention Pretty Rose? There must be something going on between Master Hakuin and Pretty Rose indeed!☺ And let's not even get into that "God – Dog" joke of Mumon!☺

Certainly, Zen Buddhism and the original Indian Buddhism are concerned with suffering. The main goal of the Buddhist teachings is to minimize suffering. Once we realize our connection with all living beings, and once we let go of some of our fears, ignorant desires, intolerance, greed, envy, unfounded pride, and some other negative feelings – we will, undoubtedly, lessen our suffering and dissatisfaction. I think that Zen Buddhism is a great remedy for dissatisfaction in life. The Indian Buddhist term for dissatisfaction and suffering is *dukkha* and it is *ku* in Japanese.

When you get no satisfaction...

Don't feel bad, just realize
That you **always** compromise!
Every single thing you do
Is not what you wanted to.

Though the means are not the same:
You want money, beauty, fame
Freedom, love, respect, or power
Something spicy, sweet, or sour...

But the goal is – **satisfaction!**
It is driving you to action
So you struggle like a beast
Persevere, strive, persist...

You work hard, yet all you get
Is predominantly – sweat!
"I can get no..." – sings the band
So you'd better understand

So you'd better: "Let it be"
And stop thinking: "ME, ME, ME"!

One of the answers of Zen Buddhism to the daily stress we experience is to live in the present moment. If you concentrate on what you are doing at the moment, rather than to always think about the tasks at hand – you will become a lot more comfortable. As Allan Watts teaches – Zen Buddhism is about becoming comfortable.

In Japan, life is really hectic and everyone is very busy. Businessmen work extra-long hours; housewives make sure their houses are clean, families are fed, pets are attended to, kids are groomed and promptly delivered to their schools and extracurricular activities; and the kids study in schools, jukus (afterschool tutoring services), learn to play the piano, go to kendo and karate classes, etc. Everyone is always in a rush, and so, Zen meditation can be a good way to calm down.

When I lived near a Buddhist temple, I saw at times people who rushed to the cemetery. They walked very quickly from their cars to the cemetery, and sometimes they almost ran to the graves they wanted to visit. Then they stood there motionless for a while – praying and contemplating. After a few minutes they ran out of the cemetery again. Why were these people in such a great hurry to pause and contemplate? How could they resume being in a hurry right after the period of contemplation and prayer? Their behavior seemed incomprehensible and puzzling to me... until I understood some of the dynamics of the Japanese society. To prosper and to be economically successful, many Japanese people try to stretch the day, but spirituality remains a part of their life and it is rarely abandoned.

Ask yourself:

1. Buddhism teaches that inner peace and harmony arise when we let go of our desires, addictions, worries, and fears. Of course we can't get rid of all of them – if we want to stay alive and well – we have to eat and drink, and even socialize. But finding some seclusion away from the noise of the daily life is often healing and comforting. Do you often go to the mountains, forests, or some other places in nature where you can stay alone for a while? Do you like to stay up at night when there is no external temptation – nothing is calling you outside of your home, because all shops are closed, and all streets are empty?

2. What is the meaning of life? Is this an important question to you?

3. Buddhism is not very concerned with the meaning of life, because of *dukkha* (*suffering*) that Buddha saw all around him. What is the meaning of all this imperfection and suffering? Buddhism doesn't seem to assume that there is any purpose for our suffering. Instead, Buddhism tells us how to get rid of suffering or at least how to decrease it.

   Personally, I believe that our imperfect life has a purpose! I believe that our desires, addictions, worries, and fears – all serve a purpose of developing us mentally and spiritually. Where do you stand on this issue?

4. Actually, "What is the meaning of wife?" – is not a silly question. To have a wife or a husband means to learn to love and to treat another person *better than oneself*. Of course marriage (or romantic partnership) often leads to parenthood – which further develops one's love and selflessness. What is the meaning of being married (or of being in a romantic partnership) for you?

5. Can you interpret the painting below, titled *The Siren*?

The Siren

On Freedom

One day an American authority on Zen – Allan Watts – came to visit Master Hakuin.

"What are the American people most proud of?" – asked Master Hakuin.

"It must be our freedom!" – answered Allan Watts. "Do the Japanese people feel free?" – he asked back.

"Like paper kites in the sky!" – replied Master Hakuin.

.   .   .   .   .

Mumon's comment:

America is only 240 years old, but Japan is an old country. Old people know that they can't become young again. When you have no youth, no beauty, no health, and are just waiting to die – what is the meaning of the word "freedom"?

The Illusion of Freedom

An Interpretation

Freedom is an important concept. People are often willing to die for freedom. No nation wants to be enslaved by another. No social class enjoys being dominated and controlled by another. Most people and most animals want to feel free and in charge of their own destiny. But are they ever free?

Can we ever avoid being who we are? If we are ignorant (and indeed most of us are ignorant in many ways) can we overcome this limitation? Of course we can study, and learn some history, literature, or science. But will it make us enlightened? Of course we can practice Zen. But will it bring us the desired liberation or the spiritual tranquility?

Can we stop the process of aging? Can we remain free of diseases? Can we stay young and strong forever? Can we choose to be beautiful? Can we find love at will? Can we always keep our friends? Can we remain in happy relationships with everyone? Can we wake up every day free of worries and sorrows? Can we stay safe and protected from harm and loss of all sorts? Can we make sure that we never lose that, which we hold dear? Can we remain excited about that, which we have obtained? Can we stay happy forever? Can we stay alive for more than a hundred years? Can we protect others from harm and loss of all sorts? Can we enjoy living in a world where all beings are happy? If we cannot – what is our freedom? What are we free to have or to experience – if we cannot experience all that?

Despite all the shortcomings and the imperfections of life, Zen Buddhism is trying to cheer us up: "Concentrate on the present moment!" "Enjoy the cup of green tea that is in your hand!" "Try to do your best!" "Don't give up easily!" "Help others as much as you can!" "See and enjoy the fleeting beauty of the things in this world!" All things decay and disappear, but new things are born and shine with their glory. Listen to the laughter of a baby and to the whispers of a bamboo forest. A frog is glad that spring time came. A cicada is calling for a mate.

Ask yourself:

Even though we are not free in life to do what we want, we can learn to enjoy doing what we can do. Some people learn to live with their disabilities. They are, of course, true heroes and heroines! Most people have to learn to live with their "disabilities" of not being very rich and of being limited by their human form. What are your "handicaps" and how well are you able to cope with them?

1. Even God is not free! God cannot be unholy, not compassionate, or not caring. God cannot give up being God. God cannot kill Himself/Herself. God cannot become evil. Similarly, good people are not free to be evil. But is this a real limitation? Is freedom the ability to do anything? If not, what is freedom?

2. On the other hand – we often enslave others without realizing it. Do you limit the sense of freedom of your spouse or your children? If so, how can you make them feel less constricted?

3. Do you have pets? If so, do you try to make them feel free? What do you think about the animals caged in the zoos, factory farms or laboratories?

Hara-kiri

"Master Hakuin, what do you think about Bushido, or the Code of the Samurai?" – asked Mondai.

"Well, what about it?" – enquired Master Hakuin.

"I mean – do you approve of it? For example, do you approve of hara-kiri – the ritual disembowelment of the dishonored samurai?" – Mondai explained the nature of his question.

"Of course I do!" – responded Master Hakuin.

"Really?!" – exclaimed Mondai in shock and disbelief. "I thought you respected life and valued it over some shady notion of honor, especially when so-called dishonor arises from disobeying one's feudal lord or failing his expectations!"

"My dear Mondai, the only hara-kiri I approve of is the act of disobeying one's hungry stomach and staying on a diet! When you get to be my age – you really have to watch your weight!" – replied Master Hakuin.

. . . . .

Mumon's comment:

Removing the fat from one's belly – shows will-power and determination. Removing the intestines from one's belly – shows blood, cut-up guts, and fecal matter.

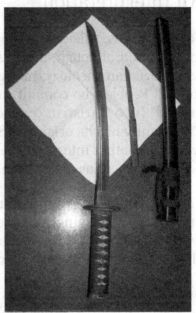

Diet

An Interpretation

For Christians, suicide is a *mortal sin. Mortal,* in this case, doesn't mean *deadly,* although suicide is undoubtedly deadly!☺ In accordance with Christian theology, mortal sin is an act which condemns one to Hell! People who commit suicide cannot be buried in a "blessed ground" (in a Christian cemetery). The condemnation of suicide in Christianity has its origins in St. Augustine's book *The City of God,* where the author interprets the Biblical commandment – *Thou shalt not kill* as meaning also – *Thou shalt not kill thyself.*

For the Japanese samurai, suicide was a sensible and honorable option, when staying alive seemed either hopeless or graceless (without honor). Japanese warriors did not believe that Gods (or Heavens) punish those who commit suicide.

According to Buddhism, life is suffering and we all should strive to escape it. Of course ending one's life by suicide is not a way to escape Samsara (the cycle of rebirths). Achieving Nirvana (permanent freedom from reincarnation) has nothing to do with killing oneself. Hence, Buddhism doesn't advocate committing suicide as a way to escape suffering.

Personally, I believe in the sanctity of life. Suicide and assisted suicide would be an acceptable option for me, only in the face of great suffering, when there is no hope for recovery. For example, if a human or an animal were experiencing the agony of a terminal disease.

For the Japanese – hara-kiri was the final challenge and the triumph over pain and suffering. "I can bear it!" – said every samurai who chose to kill himself rather than to live with disgrace.

In the story, Master Hakuin is obviously not fond of hara-kiri, because for him – life is most valuable. If one wants to prove how tough one is – he/she should chisel the mind, the body, and the spirit, instead of throwing the gift of life away. But of course this is a new understanding of values. In the feudal Japan, not life itself, but obedience and servitude – were the most appreciated values. As time passes by, our values evolve...

Ask yourself:

1. What is the highest value for you: honor, material riches, social status, respect of others, pleasure, family ties, patriotism, etc., or life itself?

2. In accordance with the original teachings of Gautama Siddhartha, life is more like a curse than like a precious gift. Although Zen Buddhism doesn't seem to view life in such dark colors, most Japanese people don't think of life as a gift from Heaven. Do you believe in the sanctity of life? Do you think that life is a precious gift?

3. When we talk about the sanctity of life, we come across a very important and controversial issue of abortion. Some people believe in the woman's right to choose, and others believe in the baby's right to life. Master Hakuin and many mystics have a solution to the issue. As medical science shows, the heart of an embryo is fully formed at the end of the 6th week from the time of conception. Most importantly – the embryo's brainwaves begin at this time. Meister Eckhart says that "God places a soul in an embryo on the 40th day from conception". If so, before the embryo can feel pain – abortion could be acceptable. But after the embryo has a fully formed and functioning heart and brainwaves – it should not be. What do you think about this solution to the issue of abortion?

4. Yukio Mishima was a Japanese writer, bodybuilder, martial-artist, and a political right-wing activist. In 1970, he chose to commit hara-kiri, as a protest against the policies of the Japanese government. In one of his interviews, Yukio Mishima expressed the view that hara-kiri was an act of preserving beauty, if a man killed himself at a young age, or when his body was still strong and healthy. Yukio Mishima died at the age of 45, when he felt that he has reached his potential in bodybuilding. Do you think that suicide can preserve beauty?

5. Is death a gate to another reality? How do you imagine afterlife?

6. In Christianity, reincarnation was originally not a foreign concept. A famous Christian scholar and theologian – Origen – was one of the proponents of reincarnation. However, Origen's teachings on reincarnation were eventually rejected by the Church. If you knew with certainty that reincarnation is true, and if you knew that some people are reborn as animals – would you still eat meat?

7. If you were to be reborn after death, where would you want to be reborn and why? Would you prefer to be born on Earth or on another planet? If on Earth, would you choose a developed, or a developing country? Would you prefer to be born far from civilization, or in the midst of it? Now, or in a distant future? Would you want to be reborn as a human being, an alien, or an animal?

8. We all must die sooner or later. Why is it better not to rush one's death?

9. Why are humans fascinated with death? Why are there so many movies and books about death? Why do people love horrors so much, that Stephen King is one of the most popular and top earning writers in the world?

10. Not only zombies are flesh eaters!☺ Can you interpret the following sculpture?

Flesh Eater

The Way of Tea

"Master Hakuin, can the tea ceremony aid a Zen practitioner in achieving satori?" – asked Mondai.

"Can a boat help a man go across the river?" – asked master Hakuin in response.

"The tea ceremony teaches to uphold the pure mind – focused on the ritual and the beauty surrounding it. The balanced and the deliberate motions of the tea master; the depth of the tea's aroma; the calm, yet, at the same time, the invigorating bouquet of flavors of the tea and the manju cookie; and finally the admiration for the potter's artistry – all lead to the realization of life's splendor and serenity." – said Master Hakuin.

"Does coffee have similar power of illumination?" – asked Mondai.

"Perhaps if you go to Starbucks!" – replied Master Hakuin.

.　　　　.　　　　.　　　　.　　　　.

Mumon's comment:

Wow! What a great commercial for Starbucks! Or was Master Hakuin just being facetious?

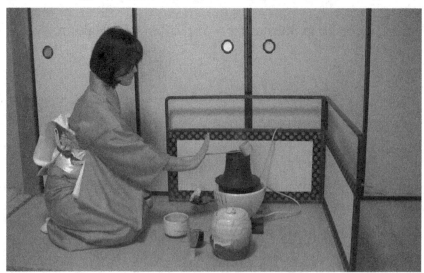

Tea Ceremony performed by Maiko Okuno

An Interpretation

The traditon of drinking green tea in Japan originated probably in the 9th century. Green tea is said to have been brought to Japan from China by a Buddhist monk – Eichu, who served it to the Emperor in the year 815. In the following year, by the order of the emperor, green tea started to be cultivated in Japan. In the 15th century, Murata Juko – who studied Zen with Master Ikkyu – changed the style of drinking tea. So far, drinking green tea had been an aristocratic custom, enjoyed in the atmosphere of luxury and opulance. Murata Juko transformed it into, what is known as, *wabi style*. Wabi (or *simplicity*) is very reminiscent of Zen principles. The tea room ought to be humble, and simple. The room should be almost empty. It may be decorated with a poem or a Zen koan, and an ikebana arrangement. Alternatively, the room may have a small window, looking out at the sky and the foliage of the nearby trees. The room should be small and dimly lit, so that the participants of the tea ceremony can focus inwardly. In this way, the tea ceremony can invoke the feeling of becoming one with nature, and thus it canlead to satori.

Later on, the green tea ceremony became also connected with the idea that "everything happens only once". "Ichi-go ichi-e" (translated as: "once in a lifetime", or "this time only") is often painted on a scroll hanging in a tea room, and it is supposed to express the Zen idea that one should treasure the present moment – which is special and different from all other moments in life. For the Westerners, this idea is resonant of "panta rhei" – the famous saying by an Ancient Greek philosopher – Heraclitus, who taught that "everything flows", and that "we cannot step in the same river twice".

Ask yourself:

Do you often think of the passing moment as a "once in a lifetime chance only"? If so, on what occassions? What moments in life do you treasure most of all?

1. Master Hakuin said: "To get the most out of life we should notice the miraculous moments of daily life." What "miraculous moments of daily life" did Master Hakuin have in mind?

2. Why do we value life more when we get older?

3. In English there is a well-known saying: "Stop and smell the roses!" What does this advice mean to you?

4. While drinking coffee may be very pleasurable, it is rarely a spiritual experience. Have you ever had a spiritual experience connected with drinking or eating? If so, on what occasion?

5. Is the Eucharist (receiving bread and wine as the symbols of Christ's body and Christ's blood) similar to a Zen tea ceremony? If so, in what sense?

6. In the 17th century Chinese tea was introduced to England. The English adopted the custom of drinking tea and turned it into much celebrated *teatime*. While the British teatime is different from the Japanese tea ceremony – both constitute important cultural events. Do you think of the English teatime as a spiritual event?

Zen and Martial Arts

"Master Hakuin, Shaolin temple is famous for its Buddhist monks practicing martial arts. On the other hand, Siddhartha Gautama Buddha was as peaceful as Jesus, Gandhi, and Mother Teresa. Is the practice of martial arts compatible with Zen Buddhism?" – asked Mondai.

"Think about it intensely today and perhaps at night you will dream the answer." – replied Master Hakuin.

Mondai did as he was told. In the morning he came to see Master Hakuin again.

"Did you have a dream related to your question?" – asked Master Hakuin.

"Yes, Master, in fact I had a very strange dream. I was the king of a small island surrounded by many other islands. Many aggressive tribes inhabited the other islands, so for our protection I ordered my people to arm themselves and practice the art of warfare. Then I saw how many of my people hardened in their spirits as a result of their military practice, and so I ordered them to renounce all violence. When they threw away their weapons, they became mild and kind again, but they also became vulnerable. So, I changed my mind and ordered them to arm themselves and prepare for warfare... I changed my mind many times and finally I woke up all sweaty and exhausted."

"And that is the answer to your question!" – said Master Hakuin and turned on his TV set to watch an action movie.

Mumon's comment:

In an imperfect and complicated world the solutions to our problems are often imperfect and complicated.

Practicing martial arts is good for the development of the body, the willpower, and self-confidence.

Practicing non-violence is good for the heart and mind. Make your own choice.

Sensei Kurobe Kazuyoshi –
4th dan, Wado Karate.

An Interpretation

In feudal Japan, during the time of samurai, there were Buddhist warrior monks called *Sohei*. These monks were the equivalent of the Teutonic Order or the Crusaders in Christianity. While normal Christian monks are expected to imitate Christ, and normal Buddhist monks are supposed to act like Buddha – these "special" monks often engaged in military conflicts and "defended" their faith by brute force.

I think that neither Christ nor Buddha would have approved of such violence! The Shaolin temple monks vow to use their martial arts only in self-defense and don't organize themselves into military units or armies. The right to self-defense is, of course, a universal human (and animal) right, but I think that the religious authorities should lead others on the path to non-violence and the ultimate compassion. Somehow, the image of monks or priests running around with guns or swords and killing people (even if they are enemies) – doesn't seem right to me.

Master Hakuin admits to watching action movies, and this to me is also a bit controversial. Should the spiritual leaders be interested in any form of violence – even if it is only simulated violence? I think that violent action and horror movies are responsible for much misery and for the cultural debasement of our societies. When children and grownups are exposed to violence on TV, at least some of them begin to glorify it and imitate it.

Why do we tell our children such horror stories as "Red Riding Hood" or "Three Blind Mice"?

Ask yourself:

1. Do you think that children should play with toy guns or other toy weapons?

2. Have you ever played with toy weapons? Did you enjoy "killing" imaginary enemies? Do you think that we should ever enjoy "killing" others in games?

3. Have you ever played violent video games? If so, was your perception of other people influenced by those games? Did you look at other people in real life and imagine shooting them (like you did in those video games)?

4. Why is there a major shortage of educational video games at the present moment? Shouldn't we use the available technology to teach history, geography, literature, art, and so on? For example, I think that a good video game would portray historical figures and historical events and allow the players to experience the past or foreign cultures. Would you like to learn history or admire modern art in video games?

5. M.M.A. (Mixed Martial Arts) events such as the *Ultimate Fighting Championship* or *Pride* (in Japan) are reminiscent of the ancient fights of gladiators. Although I personally watch them at times – I am not sure if I support them as a form of sport. They tend to promote more violence than sportsmanship. What is your opinion about these events?

6. In the past, intellectuals were usually weak and not focused on their bodies Nowadays the image of an intellectual (such as a writer, a university professor, a doctor, an artist, or a politician) is somewhat changing. Already mentioned in this book, Japanese writer – Yukio Mishima was also a bodybuilder. Ernest Hemingway was not only a writer, but also a boxer. Nonetheless, intellectual prowess doesn't usually go hand in hand with physical prowess. Why not?

7. Is there a connection between having a tidy room and a well-built or a well-taken-care-of body? If so, what is it?

Fight for our Earth!

The Path of No Desires

"Master Hakuin, is it possible to overcome all desires?" – asked Matte.

"Of course it is!" – responded Master Hakuin. "Look in the garden! Can you see the Buddha statue there? – he asked.

"Yes, I can see it." – replied Matte.

"Does the statue have any desires?" – asked Master Hakuin.

"I suppose it doesn't." – replied Matte.

"Be like the statue!" – said Master Hakuin and went for dinner.

.   .   .   .   .

Mumon's comment:

Master Hakuin is very optimistic. He hopes that Matte will eventually understand that he is not made of stone.

An Interpretation

One day, Gautama Siddhartha decided to sit under a sacred fig tree (known as the Bodhi Tree) until he could understand how to break free from the cycle of suffering. He was resolved to keep meditating, until he could understand what life was all about. When Gautama Siddhartha sat under the Bodhi Tree, he was challenged by Mara, the Demon God of Desires. Mara shot the arrows of desires at Gautama, but Gautama remained seated and unmoved. The arrows changed into flowers and fell harmlessly on Gautama. Finally Lord Mara gave up and left. At that moment, Gautama became enlightened, and from then on he has become known as *the Buddha*.

When I was about eighteen years old, I had many questions about life. Was there any purpose to my life or to anyone's life? Why was I alive? What was the best way to live? What ethics should I follow? Should I be egoistic or helpful to others? Should I seek my own happiness or the happiness of others? What would make me truly happy?

I asked many people, and I consulted some books – but I still couldn't find any satisfying answers. Finally, I decided to lie down on the floor in my room and wait until I receive some answers. I remained motionless for many hours. Then, Lord Mara appeared and shot his arrows at me. The arrows didn't turn into flowers, like they did for the Buddha. They hit me hard, instead, and entered my body deeply.

The first was the arrow of stiffness. I felt stiff and painful from staying motionless for so long. Some parts of my body felt numb, since I haven't turned for hours. My blood circulation was severely compromised, and I began to feel an overwhelming desire to move...

The second arrow of Mara was the arrow of hunger. The arrow entered my stomach through the nostrils, just as the aroma of my mother's dinner arrived from the adjacent room. The dinner was being served in the dining room, and my stomach began to sound an alarm. The aroma of the freshly cooked pancakes made them really hard to resists...

The third and the final arrow of Mara shot me through the ear! It was my father calling me to join everyone at the dinner table. I couldn't refuse my father and ignore this most consequential arrow of Lord Mara...

When Lord Mara's arrows penetrated my body – suddenly I got the answers! A voice inside me said: "NOW JUST GET UP AND LIVE! Eat, drink, move your body and escape the pain! Accept your social circumstances. Seek pleasure and satisfaction and avoid discomfort! Then..." – the voice continued – "understand that all beings have the same desires, and just like you – they suffer! Thus, live in such a way that you don't hurt others. Make others feel happy – whenever you can do it, and at the very least try not to make them suffer! "Others" – means all living beings, not only your friends and family! Follow these basic principles, and you won't be lost!"

And so, I got up from the floor. From that time, I have become more concerned with the plight of others. Compassionate vegetarianism has become the path of my life. Lord Mara had showed me the way!

Ask yourself:

1. Are there good and bad desires? If you think so, name a few good desires and a few bad ones.

2. Which desires nurture the shallow identity of the self (as a person who is separated and different from the rest of the world), and which desires help us discover the deep identity (as an expression of the Universal Energy)?

3. Should a human being try to ignore or suppress his or her desires to eat, drink, sleep, etc.? What are the physical and spiritual dangers of asceticism?

4. Should a human being indulge in his or her desires to eat, drink and sleep to the point of gluttony and slothfulness? What are the physical and spiritual dangers of gluttony and slothfulness?

5. Is there a way not to be too anxious about the world, and at the same time not to be indifferent about the world? Why should we try to remain calm, yet interested in changing the world into a better place?

6. Hate is a desire to make someone unhappy. Compassionate love (unselfish love) is a desire to make someone happy. Why the former one is a bad desire and the latter one is a good desire? Why should we seek to eradicate hatred and develop compassion?

7. Should we cherish the desire to preserve life? If so, why?

A Quiet Pond

Is this Master Hakuin's Temple?

When a new disciple arrived at Master Hakuin's temple, he found Master Hakuin sitting on a bench in the garden.

"Hello!" – said the disciple – "I am looking for Master Hakuin's temple. Is this it?" – he asked.

"No, it isn't!" – answered Master Hakuin. "But, please, do enter!" – he added.

.   .   .   .   .

Mumon's comment:

Does a temple, a house, a piece of land, or a mountain belong to you, or do you perhaps belong to them?

When white people arrived in North America, they thought of the land as their private property and began to fence it off. Native North Americans had never imagined such an idea. In their minds the land did not belong to them, but rather they belonged to the land.

Someone is clearly SELFISH here!

An Interpretation

Mumon's comment explains the main point of this story. Human beings are guests on this planet and ought to walk lightly on it. Instead, they often claim ownership of everything they see. Animals, plants, minerals, gas, oil, land, and water – are all claimed as human property or as "natural resources" that ought to be harvested. Do the forests belong to us any more than they belong to the bears, wolves, or deer? Do the oceans belong to us any more than they belong to the fish, crabs, lobsters, or dolphins? If the forest animals fenced off their forests and if the water animals fenced off their oceans and seas – how could humans survive? If any species of animals thought of us as their "food resource" – wouldn't we fight against them? But might does not make it right! Just because we have the power over other species on this planet – it doesn't mean that we should kill off or enslave other beings and destroy their natural habitats!

Big companies claim ownership of everything they can. Rich people buy land and bodies of water – and forbid other people to enter their "private properties". Master Hakuin doesn't believe in such "justice". How about you?

Ask yourself:

1. Many Christians claim that the Bible supports the idea of man's ownership of land, flora, and fauna. They say that God created humans and all the creatures on Earth to be used as our resources. But Jesus is often compared to a good shepherd, who "rejoices when a lost sheep is found again". Does a good shepherd imprison and kill his sheep? What should be our role as stewards on this planet?

2. When chemical factories pollute rivers and springs and people can't drink unprocessed water anymore, who should pay for the bottled water: the chemical factories or the private citizens?

After the Fukushima nuclear accident in 2011 many people in Japan lost their homes, but haven't been compensated for it. Although the news is hushed up and not reported by the Japanese government – many people got sick as a result of the nuclear pollution. Every year, the Japanese float lanterns down the rivers to honor the family members who had recently passed away. In the last two years (2012 and 2013) all floating lanterns got quickly sold out. There are simply more deceased than the market (lantern producers) expected! Should the power company – TEPCO (Tokyo Electric Power Company) compensate the people for the loss of their homes? Should TEPCO financially assist those who developed cancer as a result of the Fukushima disaster? While the Japanese are usually a patient and obedient nation, Western people are less accepting of mismanagement of big corporations and the government cover-ups. Hence, 75 American sailors of USS Raegan who were involved in the rescue efforts after Fukushima accident and who developed leukemia, brain tumors and testicular cancer – are presently suing TEPCO. (For further information see – *Charles Bonner lawsuit* on the Internet.)

Not the Messenger

One day, a Harvard professor visited Master Hakuin in his temple. After the tea ceremony, the professor said:

"Master Hakuin, I hear that you understand Zen Buddhism well and that your teachings are quite popular. But I also hear that you are mostly self-taught. Do you have any formal credentials to teach Zen?"

Master Hakuin replied:

"Does a swallow need any formal credentials to fly?"

.   .   .   .   .

Mumon's comment:

Bruce Lee said:

"Don't concentrate on the finger pointing to the moon, or you will lose all the heavenly glory!"

Focus on the message rather than on the messenger!

.   .   .   .   .

Edward's comment:

I have no credentials either, yet I was allowed to place a comment in this book! Nice!

An Interpretation

We often place much emphasis on references, credentials, and opinions of other people. But the greatest teachers in the history of human race boldly stated their own truths, often contradicting their predecessors, rather than seeking their approval or ideological support.

For example, Jesus said that the Law of Moses – "An eye for an eye, and a tooth for a tooth" – was to be discarded, and instead, the Law of the Ultimate Compassion should be followed – "If they strike you on one cheek, let them strike you on the other."

Siddhartha Gautama Buddha disagreed with the accepted religious dogmas of his day and offered his own teachings.

So did Mohammed, and all the other great spiritual leaders, who established new religions and/or belief systems.

"When it comes to understanding the world and its laws and choosing the best possible belief – we should follow no one, but the truth itself." – Socrates taught his students. Of course Socrates was a pretty smart guy, and it is good that he believed in the very same idea that we are proposing right now! We don't need any authorities or credentials to back us up, but if they happen to do so – that's fine too!☺

Ask yourself:

1. While formal credentials are often irrelevant to one's actual state of knowledge and understanding of some matter, we like to see some external proofs that the person we are listening to had spent a considerable amount of time and effort studying the matter he or she is speaking about. Why?

2. Some political leaders (such as presidents and prime ministers) may have studied in renowned educational institutions (such as Harvard, Yale, etc.), yet they may possess no wisdom to lead

their societies to real prosperity. How can we make sure that we elect the right political leaders?

3. Socrates and Plato advised that rulers should be elected from among trained thinkers and philosophers. Do you think that trained intellectuals – such as Vaclav Havel (the prime minister of the Czech Republic) are better suited as country leaders than the members of rich and powerful families (or actors ☺) who traditionally win the elections in many modern "democracies"?

4. What qualities should a political or spiritual leader possess?

5. Do you often vote for political leaders? If so, on what basis do you choose whom to vote for? Are the programs of modern political leaders usually clearly stated, or are the present day governments elected on the basis of misleading advertising and political spinning?

6. Do you think that older people are better suited to govern countries than young people? If so, why?

7. Could you be a good political, social or religious leader? If so, why? If not, why not?

No Pilot License!...

The Artistic Vagueness

"Which of my Zen stories do you like the best?" – Master Hakuin asked the venerable Master Zensei.

"I like one of them best... I can't remember the title." –replied the venerable Master Zensei, who was getting to be quite old and somewhat senile.

"Really? Our preferences are so similar!" – responded Master Hakuin.

.   .   .   .   .

Mumon's comment:

Being flexible, Master Hakuin leaves the interpretation of the story to the readers. Of course Zen stories are always only as good as their readers.

An Interpretation

I think that Mumon is onto something interesting here. The most popular works of art seem to be those that can be interpreted in accordance with the preferences and the wishes of the audience. For example, Franz Kafka's famous book *The Trial* can be interpreted in accordance with one's own beliefs, and because of this flexibility it becomes a magical book. It is also true for other great, mysterious literary works, such as *The Stranger* by Albert Camus, *Hunger* by Knut Hamsun, *Thus Spoke Zarathustra* by Friedrich Nietzsche, and even *The Little Prince* by Antoine de Saint-Exupéry. They all can be understood in many ways.

The more mystery there is in a book (or a movie, painting, sculpture, musical composition, ballet performance, etc.) – the more wisdom can be found in it by the readers (or the viewers and listeners). In fact, a smart, observant, and creative person can read poems in passing clouds and philosophical treatises in tea leaves. We are surrounded by the mystery of life and in any element of life we can discover the entire Universe!

Is this what the story about artistic vagueness is about? Or is it just about senility and old age? Or perhaps Master Zensei doesn't like any of the stories of Master Hakuin and this is why his answer is so vague?

Ask yourself:

1. What does it mean: "When the student is ready – the teacher appears"?

2. What does it mean: "Beauty is in the eyes of the beholder"?

3. Paintings by Marc Chagall, Salvatore Dali, Zdzisław Beksiński, or even Vincent Van Gogh – reflect the inner worlds of their creators. They are not trying to show any objective reality. Do you like such paintings? If so, why?

4. Artistic vagueness often turns the audience into artists. One of the results of practicing Zen Buddhism is becoming a thinker and a philosopher. Zen Buddhism doesn't offer clear answers, but only hints at them. Are you an artist at heart? If so, Zen is for you!

5. What are the dangers of too much vagueness in a message? The Biblical Commandment: "Thou shall not kill!" can be interpreted as "Thou shall not kill people!" or as "Thou shall not kill sentient beings!" Which interpretation is the correct one? Are you sure that your choice is correct? If so, on what basis?

6. What does it mean to speak like a diplomat? Why are politicians often vague in their answers? Are you usually diplomatic in discussions with other people?

7. In Japan, people rarely say: "no" and refuse anything openly. Instead, they usually say: "maybe". For example, when someone is asked: "Will you visit me someday soon?" and the answer is: "Thank you for the invitation. Let me think about it" – it is a form of refusal. This unclear way of talking is the result of Confucian politeness and the riddle style of Zen teachings. Do you prefer when other people are polite and vague, or when they are bluntly honest (to the point of being rude) in conversations with you?

8. Can you interpret the rock painting titled *"Life"* (on the previous page)?

Zen - Healed

"Sitting in Zazen hurts my knees and my back too much. I can't bear it!" – complained Atarashin during the meditation.

At that moment Master Hakuin shouted: "Zen – Pain!" and he struck Atarashin on his shoulder with a bamboo stick so hard that all the demons left Atarashin's body and got into a herd of swine, which then ran into a lake and drowned.

Atarashin instantly achieved satori.

.   .   .

Mumon's comment:

If you can walk to heaven on painful legs... or even crawl there – the gates will be wide open!

By the way, did the pigs really have to die in that story?!

An Interpretation

It's a pity that so many stories, even those about great compassion, have images of death and horror. Why did the great story of Jesus healing a man possessed by evil spirits have to show animals as victims of this action?

I guess it's because we are fascinated with horror. Horror stories wake us up and make us pay attention. This is why 90% of the movies we can see on TV portray violence. Even TV news is usually about violence, death, and destruction.

Did Little Red Riding Hood have to be eaten by a wolf? Did rescuing Red Riding Hood and her grandma require killing the wolf and ripping open its stomach? Don't such gory stories for children have a negative impact on their psyche? Of course they do!

I know, because I was one of those kids whose psyche was damaged by horror stories for kids. When I was 4 or 5 years old, I suddenly started to cry while pointing at an empty corner of the room: "Mommy, mommy, look there! The wolves are going to eat the bunny!" Since there was nothing in the corner to which I was pointing, my mom became worried and took me to a psychiatrist. The doctor diagnosed me as an "oversensitive child", and told my mom to stop me from watching or listening to any fairytales "for at least 6 months" – he said. "Otherwise the boy may become either a genius or a madman" – the doctor added dramatically. And... I became the latter.☺

Mumon is quite right to be angry at that unfortunate mention of the swine drowning in a lake. But why did Atarashin achieve satori from a hard blow of a Zen stick? Perhaps because he understood that success requires struggle and hard work...

When we go to the gym and exercise – we feel pain, but we keep enduring it in order to achieve physical prowess. In order to achieve mental prowess – we spend long and exhausting hours studying, watching the news, reading books, etc. In order to achieve spiritual prowess – we must endure the pain of long hours of meditation, contemplation and self-evaluation. It requires much time and effort to try to understand what life is about. It is a very frustrating and painful road. But the higher mountains we climb – the more we get to see. Perhaps it is so.

Ask yourself:

1. How much time and energy do you devote each day to improving your mind, body, and spirit?

2. Is helping others a good way to develop your compassion? Is it important to be compassionate? If so, why?

3. Are you good at enduring pain and hardships in life? As a popular proverb states: "When the going gets tough, the tough get going!" Are you tough enough? How can we improve our endurance?

4. "As long as our culture accepts bloodshed as heroic or necessary in order to survive, we will continue to have wars." Do you agree with this statement?

The Buddha and the Elephant

One day, Master Hakuin went to a Buddhist conference in Thailand. When he arrived at the temple where the conference was being held, there was a big Buddha statue in front of it. Many masters gathered in front of the statue to pay their respects, but Master Hakuin passed by the statue and went a bit further. A gray female elephant was chained to a tree nearby. Master Hakuin came up to the elephant and said:

"Greetings to you, my Teacher! I brought you a bunch of bananas!"

.   .   .   .   .

Mumon's comment:

A statue made of stone or a living elephant – who is closer to Buddha? The choice is easy!

In order to test his invention of the electric chair, Thomas Edison electrocuted many animals: dogs, cats, cows, horses, and even an elephant. How can Western people think of him as a genius?

An Interpretation

The main form of Buddhism practiced in Thailand is Theravada Buddhism, not Zen. It is said that Theravada Buddhists are primarily concerned with achieving a state of liberation or blissful happiness, whereas Mahayana Buddhists (and Zen is a part of the Mahayana tradition) are said to be more concerned with helping other beings achieve liberation. This is of course a great simplification of things, because every practitioner of Buddhism has his or her own goal or goals in mind. Some Theravada Buddhists want to help others and some Mahayana Buddhists are focused only on their own liberation. Anyway, perhaps because of their Theravada background, the monks in the story are more concerned with paying their respect to the image of the Buddha chiseled in stone, than with the plight of a live animal chained nearby. Master Hakuin, on the other hand, is mostly concerned with the well-being of a fellow sentient creature.

The elephants in Thailand don't look very happy. Tourists can see them easily, because elephants are used to offer exotic rides and photo opportunities. After walking back and forth with tourists on their backs all day long, the elephants spend their nights chained to the trees. In nature, elephants are very unselfish and highly social animals. Sadly, in captivity they have no social life and no freedom at all. Hence, it is strange and ironic to see the Buddha statues (which to my mind are synonymous with compassion) all around in Thailand, right next to the miserable elephants...

It is ironic that elephants are not treated well in a very Buddhist country, because elephants play an important role in the Buddhist tradition. For example, we are told that before Gautama Siddhartha was born, his mother had a dream that a white elephant gave her a lily and entered her body through her side. This dream was interpreted by the fortunetellers, and the birth of either a very powerful ruler or an enlightened person (Buddha) was foretold. Furthermore, when Gautama Siddhartha became enlightened, he formulated his teachings as *the Four Noble Truths*, which he said were "like the footprints of an elephant."

It's particularly ironic that elephants are not well treated in Thailand, where the elephant is chosen to be the country's national animal. An image of an elephant was at some point placed on the national flag of Thailand and used as the official seal of the king. While the divine three-headed elephant Erawan is said to carry God Indra, the real elephants of flesh and bones carry tourists (or sometimes dance and perform other tricks) and are just treated as money-making machines.

On a positive note, I am glad to say that stray dogs are usually treated much better in some parts of Thailand than in most Asian countries. In South Korea, China, Vietnam, and many other Asian countries, dogs and cats are eaten, and all strays are usually petrified of people. In Thailand (at least in Phuket), stray dogs get fed by people and are welcome near the bars and the restaurants, in the parks, on the beaches, and even inside the stores. In Japan, dogs and cats are not eaten, but dogs are rarely kept indoors and spend their lives usually on chains.

Thomas Edison electrocuted many animals to test his horrible invention – the electric chair, and to discourage the use of AC current (invented by his competitors), in favor of his DC current. He was not the only "genius" to act cruelly to animals...

An elephant and a Buddha statue in Thailand

Ask yourself:

1. What does the word "genius" mean to you? Can a person be both – devoid of common sense, and at the same time endowed with brilliance?

2. Are the zoo animals happy? Do you prefer to watch animals in vivid computer simulations, or do you prefer to see them locked up in cages? Is it a good idea to abolish zoos?

3. What is more important to you – an ant or a temple? Explain your choice.

4. If you were an ant, what would you think of human beings?☺

5. How can you interpret the following cartoon by F. Bacon?

6. Is there anything an elephant can teach a human being?

The Buddha and the Elephant

The Best Belief

Master Hakuin asked the venerable Master Zensei:

"Master, tell me what Buddhism has taught you!"

The venerable Master Zensei replied:

"Life is suffering. Suffering is caused by attachments and desires. Meditation is the path to rid oneself of attachments and desires. The goal of practicing Buddhism is Nirvana – a state of non-attachment and non-desire, which stops the cycle of rebirths and ends all suffering."

"But if life is suffering, then are we here as punishment or by mistake?" – asked master Hakuin.

"Perhaps the world is just an accident of nature?" – replied the venerable Master Zensei.

"It is a sad belief!" – commented Master Hakuin. "Is it possible to imagine a happier one? For example that life on the whole is good, and the purpose of life is enjoyment and learning?"

"But how would we know that such a belief is true?" – asked the venerable Master Zensei.

"We could not be sure, but if all beliefs are possible – then we should choose the happiest one!" – responded Master Hakuin.

"I believe that it is time for dinner!" – said the venerable Master Zensei, and both of them hurried to the dining room.

.   .   .   .   .

Mumon's comment:

Is God good? Is God evil?

Or is there no God at all?

Choose the most beneficial belief, and don't miss your dinner!

An Interpretation

Sensei in Japanese means *teacher* or *master*. Hence, the name *Zensei* may be a contraction of two words: *Zen* and *sensei* – meaning: *teacher of Zen*. Furthermore, in Japanese the word: *zensei* has its own meaning, which is: *previous incarnations*. Finally, the name Zensei may refer to the main character of the book by Giselle Ladines titled *Zensei's Stories*.

In the above story, Master Zensei is a proponent of the classical Buddhist view that life is suffering. However, Master Hakuin wants to subscribe to a happier philosophy.

In the history of Western Philosophy, the idea of choosing the best possible belief is known as *Pascal's Wager*. Blaise Pascal was a French philosopher, who proposed that it is safer and potentially far more profitable to lead a life of a good Christian, rather than to reject Christianity. According to Pascal, if a person lives a pious Christian life, he or she may have to sacrifice a bit of fun in this life (for example, he or she cannot live in debauchery, has to go to church every Sunday, etc.), but may potentially gain eternity in Heaven in the afterlife. On the other hand, if a person rejects Christianity – he or she may have a bit more fun in this life, but may possibly end up in Hell for eternity in the afterlife. Pascal believed that this reasoning proves beyond a shadow of a doubt that it is much more profitable to be a devout Christian.

Personally, I am not convinced that Pascal had it right, because his premises are questionable. Is it really necessary to go to church every Sunday in order to go to Heaven? If Christian God exists – will He not welcome Mahatma Gandhi or Buddha in Heaven?

Nonetheless, the idea of choosing the best belief sounds sensible to me. Nothing about life seems certain. Hence, why should we not choose the most empowering belief? Some people believe in God and others believe that God doesn't exist. None of these beliefs can be verified. But believing in a benevolent God is much more empowering and hopeful than believing that we are some freaks or mistakes of nature. Master Hakuin chooses to believe that life is not just a painful error, which we must try to get out of, but that life is ultimately good and purposeful.

Ask yourself:

1. Do you believe that life is ultimately good? If so, why? If not, why not?

2. If God, or the Divine Energy, created life – what is the purpose of it?

3. If Heaven and Hell exist – where would Buddha and Mahatma Gandhi end up and why do you think so?

4. If you could imagine the afterlife and it would come true – what would your imagined, ideal afterlife look like?

5. If you are an atheist – you believe that after we die we become only fertilizer. Is the belief in fertilizer an empowering belief? Does it make you happy? Could you find inspiration in the words: "In Fertilizer we trust!", or: "May Fertilizer bless you!"?☺

Justice

"Master Hakuin, we often see that a good man dies and a bad man thrives. Is there justice in the world?" – asked Mondai.

"When you help others – you help yourself, and when you hurt others – you hurt yourself!" – replied Master Hakuin.

.   .   .   .   .

Mumon's comment:

The World is an Ocean of beings. Each being perceives itself as a separate entity, a separate drop of water... until it realizes that it is a part of the Ocean.

When you hurt another – you hurt yourself!

293

And then there are also sharks!...

An Interpretation

When we look at life around us, it is difficult to imagine that there is justice in the world. We see so many innocent children and animals suffering cruel fates. Children suffer from diseases, accidents, poverty, hunger, violence, and abuse at the hands of adults. Animals are tortured in the name of human science, or imprisoned and slaughtered for food. We see good people - who are kind and gentle to others - hurt physically and emotionally and stricken by misfortunes of all sorts. How can their suffering ever be erased or undone? Even if those innocent beings finally find respite in death and perhaps also in afterlife (in heaven or in their next incarnations), it still doesn't seem fair that they had to suffer with no fault of their own, and often due to the wrongdoing of others. It seems that their suffering for "the sins of others" can never be regarded as just... unless... the world is a Single Being!

Imagine that the body parts of a single person think of themselves as separate beings. A man is walking in a forest. Suddenly, his eyes make a poor judgment and his feet trip over a root. The man tumbles down on a rock and breaks his wrist. His eyes made a poor judgment, his feet stepped wrongly, but his "innocent" wrist is broken. In separation, the wrist did not make any mistakes and is suffering for the "sins of others". The wrist suffers for the wrongdoing of the eyes and the feet. If each body part thinks of itself as a separate being – it seems that there is no justice. But of course we know better. We know that all the body parts of the man belong to a single person, and that his fall resulting in a broken wrist (although unfortunate) cannot be thought of as unjust.

If all beings are interconnected – no one is innocent. Of course we wish that there was no suffering in the world regardless of the reasons for it. But if we believe in the Oneness of the World – at least we can preserve our sense of justice.

Ask yourself:

1. If your beloved son were a murderer, would you want him to suffer for what he had done, or would you prefer to simply prevent him (by incarceration) from any further wrongdoing? Should a penal system seek retribution for the suffering of the victims, or should it simply seek to prevent any reoccurrence of the crime? If you believe in the latter – should there be the death penalty? Canada and most countries in the world have abolished the death penalty. China, North Korea, Iraq, Iran, United States, Japan and a few other countries still uphold the death penalty. Are you opposed to or in favor of the death penalty?

2. When Jesus was tortured by his executioners he turned to God and said: "Forgive them Father, for they don't know what they are doing!" Do the criminals ever know what they are doing? Should we pity all criminals? (Of course even if we pity them, we have a moral obligation to stop them from harming others!)

3. What do you think of the idea of *global* or *communal karma*? Is the society responsible for the beliefs and behavior of its members? Do we bear responsibility for the sins of our children, if we teach them the wrong values?

4. If we are all interconnected and all One – is there any meaning in envy, hatred, intolerance, discrimination, greed, and most other vices?

Solidarity

"How much do you care for the Japanese people?" – Master Hakuin asked the foreigner.

"I think of them as my brothers and sisters!" – answered the foreigner.

"Were you in Japan when the Fukushima nuclear power plant accident took place?" – asked Master Hakuin.

"Yes, I was." – answered the foreigner.

"And did you leave Japan right after the accident, like most foreigners did?" – asked Master Hakuin.

"No, I did not." – responded the foreigner.

"Why did you stay?" – inquired Master Hakuin.

"Out of solidarity with the Japanese people who couldn't escape to live in another country. They had to stay and suffer the consequences. So, I did the same." – said the foreigner.

"And do you regret your decision?" – asked Master Hakuin. "I know that you have cancer now... which might have been caused by the exposure to the radiation." – he added quietly.

"Yes, I am sick with cancer." – said the foreigner. "But whether I recover or not – I did the right thing. God will decide my fate."

"You have become a Zen master!" – said Master Hakuin to the foreigner and bowed.

.　　　.　　　.　　　.　　　.

Mumon's comment:

Zen is like travelling through a wormhole. It may not always be safe, but it is direct and fast!

A single pebble affects the whole lake!

An Interpretation

In the twentieth century, the word "solidarity" became synonymous with the struggle of the Polish workers against the oppression of the communist government of Poland. Thanks to an unprecedented support of the vast majority of Polish people for the *Solidarity Workers' Union*, and thanks to the wisdom of Mr. Gorbachev (who brought about "glasnost" and "perestroika" in the Soviet Union) – Poland became a free country.

But the Polish people are not the only ones who can show solidarity for their fellowmen. In fact, the Japanese people are also well known for being great team players.

In the aftermath of the Fukushima power plant disaster, many foreigners left Japan in a hurry. However, some have stayed, and some of them had to pay the price for this show of solidarity with the Japanese society.

It is pointless to speculate whether those foreigners who have stayed in Japan after the Fukushima accident were on the higher moral grounds than those who have left. It was a personal choice of each individual and it depended on various factors, including how long one had lived in Japan prior to the disaster, what were one's social ties with the Japanese people, what was one's job contract, accommodations, etc.

On the other hand, solidarity in suffering has its merits, as it clearly shows compassion and care for the others fellow beings.

Ask yourself:

1. Here is what modern philosophers call a "thought experiment" designed to discover if you are prejudiced against other races, or if you are truly bias-free:

    Imagine that you are passing by a river, and you notice two children struggling in water and crying for help. One child is of your own nation – you can hear the child crying for help in your native language. The other child is crying out in a foreign language, but you understand that this child is also crying for help. Which child will you help first and why?

Do you take into consideration the age of the children, their gender, the distance of each child from you, etc., or is the kids' nationality your primary concern? Try to be honest with yourself and think what factors you would take into consideration.

2. Jesus said: "There is no one who has left his brothers, sisters, mother, father, (or) children for me and the gospel, who will not receive hundred times as many brothers, sisters, mothers, fathers, (and) children." (Mark 10:30) Do we have a greater moral obligation to protect our own children over the children of strangers? If so, why? [Actually our moral obligation may come from the fact that our own children have greater expectations from us than from anyone else.]

3. Globalization, interracial marriages, and the fusion of the world's cultures, religions, and ideologies – are a fact. Are you a citizen of the world?

Is Zen Buddhism Happy?

The original Indian Buddhism holds that life is suffering, but the Japanese traditional religion was Shintoism. In Shintoism all beings are the manifestations of the Divine – all are Children of God. The rocks, the mountains, the rivers, the trees, the animals, and the humans – are all very precious and should be appreciated. While Zen adopted some ideas from the original Indian Buddhism, it grew in the soil of Shintoism. Hence, Zen is a happy philosophy filled with humor, and the Japanese are mostly happy people... Or anyway they should be!☺

An Interpretation

On the whole, Gautama's philosophy of seeing life as suffering and hoping to escape it – is quite different from the Japanese Zen Buddhism. Zen grew out in the environment of Shintoism – a religion which recognizes beauty and value in all the elements of the world. The rivers, the trees, the rocks, and all the animals – are the manifestations of God and are very valuable. In Shintoism, suffering does not undermine the value of life, and in fact it has its use. Suffering has a cleansing power. Japanese Bushido code requires a samurai to cleanse his disgrace by suffering in the act of disembowelment – seppuku. Since suffering has its use, it must also be respected. Zen Buddhism doesn't view suffering as the ultimate evil. Perhaps this is why Zen doesn't look for a way to escape life, but instead, it teaches how to live to the fullest. Zen teaches how to concentrate on the present moment, and indeed how to "squeeze the juice out of life".

The story titled *Is Zen Buddhism Happy?* brings the reader back to the very first story in the book, titled *Famous Quotes*. In the first *Zen-Zen* story Master Hakuin asks his pupil what is better: to be or not to be? While the original Indian Buddhism chooses non-existence, Zen Buddhism sounds a resounding YES to life. At least this is how I see it.

Ask yourself:

1. Would you describe yourself as a happy person? If you are not very happy (because happiness passes by quickly, and because we suffer much during the course of life), what can you do to make your life happier?

2. What have you learnt from this book about the nature of happiness? (If nothing at all – consider reading it again!☺)

3. In the Greek mythology, Sisyphus tries to push a rock to the top of a mountain, but before he manages to complete his task, the rock rolls down the mountain and Sisyphus has to start

again from the bottom. Sisyphus endlessly tries to reach his goal and endlessly fails to do so. In his book – *The Myth of Sisyphus* – Albert Camus compares human existence to the plight of Sisyphus. According to Camus, human existence is fraught with failure and disappointment, yet, we always try to "push the rock to the top of the mountain" and create a world filled with sense and order. Camus tells us that the world is filled with absurdity and chaos, and in fact, it is heroic to act like Sisyphus and to try to make sense of this unreliable and ever-changing world.

What are the ways to create some reliability and order in the world of constant change and uncertainty? What can you do in your daily life to reassure others, and to make others feel safer and more confident in life? Is Zen a good way to reject existential angsts?

4. Can true happiness be achieved in isolation? Can you be truly happy knowing that many other beings suffer? Is helping others a way to achieve one's own happiness?

Why This Book

"Master Hakuin, why did you write this book?" – asked Mumon.

"For money, fame, and power!" – answered Master Hakuin.

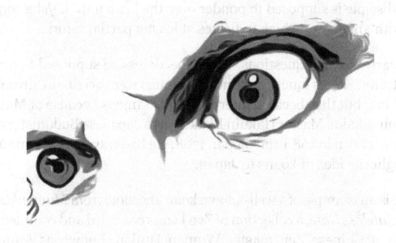

Sayonara!

Koans and Visual Koans

A traditional Zen koan consists of a short question or an anecdote. A question such as: "What is the sound of one hand clapping?", or "Does a dog have Buddha-nature?" is given to the student by his/her master. The disciple is supposed to ponder over the koan until he/she comes up with an answer which indicates at least a partial satori.

Similarly to Koan questions, Koan anecdotes are supposed to make you think. Koans (questions and anecdotes) were originally invented in China, but they became internationally famous because of Master Hakuin Ekaku. Master Hakuin Ekaku was a Japanese Buddhist monk who was born in 1686 and died in 1768. He had traveled to China and brought the idea of koans to Japan.

Here is an example of a well-known koan anecdote from *Mumonkan – The Gateless Gate*, a collection of Zen koans compiled and commented on by a Chinese Zen master Wumen Huikai, known as Mumon (1183-1260):

Three people are looking at a flag moving in the wind. Two of them are students and one man is their master. One of the students says: "The flag is moving". The other student says: "No, no! Actually it is not the flag. It is the wind that is moving the flag! The wind is moving." Then the master says: "It is not the wind. It is not the flag. It is the mind that is moving".

So what does it mean?

The world of experiences is inside one's mind. It is up to you to see the beauty or the ugliness in the world around you. If you see the beauty – it is there! If you see something as ugly – it is. If you see something as interesting – it is. And so on. Everything is the way one sees it. Of course, the external reality stimulates you to perceive the beauty or to perceive the ugliness, and it changes your perception to some degree. On the other hand, you can also try to control the way you see things. You can try to perceive things in the way that makes you happy. You can see everything in a positive way.

Here is a set of visual koans designed by Master Hakuin of *Zenzen Stories*. A visual koan consists of a picture and a word. This collage is meant to make one think and open one's mind.

Whenever you want to challenge your creativity, or you want to ponder upon the nature of life – select one of the visual koans and try to understand its meaning. Also try to give your own title to each picture and see if you can come up with interesting and telling combinations.

Human in Nature	Power of Diligence	Childhood
Truth	Vices	Optimism
Pessimism	Love without Boundaries	Real Medicine

307

Diet	Art	Motherhood
Insecurity	Life	Wisdom
Questions and Answers	Self	Responsibility

 Society	False Assumption	 Crime and Suffering
 Recurrence of Life	 Roots	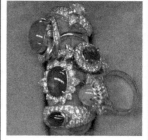 Vanity
Analytical Science	Transformation	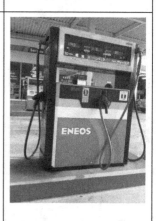 Blood

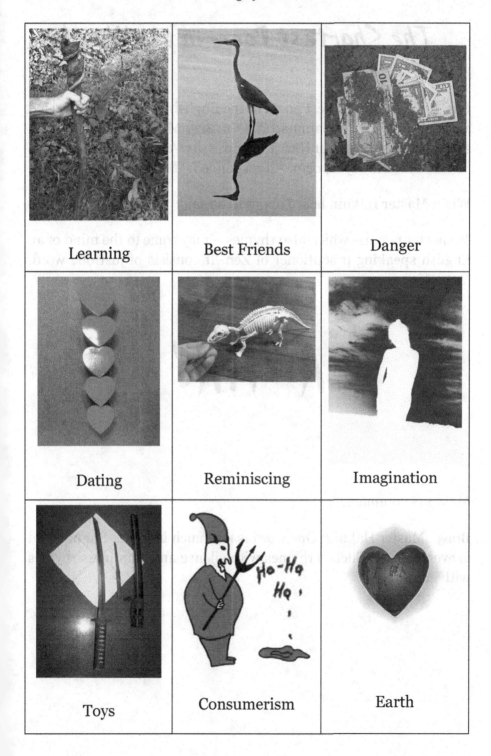

Learning

Best Friends

Danger

Dating

Reminiscing

Imagination

Toys

Consumerism

Earth

The Shortest Poem in the World

It is said that the shortest poem in the English language was created and delivered by Muhammad Ali. In 1975 Muhammad Ali gave a speech to the students at Harvard University. At the end of the speech he was asked to say a poem. Ali responded: "Me, We!"

When Master Hakuin heard about it, he said:

"A shorter poem – which also rhymes – may come to the mind of an English speaking practitioner of Zen. It consists of just one word: "A-ha!""

A-HA!

.   .   .   .   .

Mumon's comment:

Bravo, Master Hakuin! One word is not much indeed... But no word is even shorter! Silence rhymes with silence and emptiness rhymes with emptiness!

The Three Jewels of Buddhism:

The Buddha, the Sangha, and the Dharma!